The law of rentcharges (commonly called chief rents), mainly from a conveyancing standpoint.

J. M. Easton

The Making of Modern Law collection of legal archives constitutes a genuine revolution in historical legal research because it opens up a wealth of rare and previously inaccessible sources in legal, constitutional, administrative, political, cultural, intellectual, and social history. This unique collection consists of three extensive archives that provide insight into more than 300 years of American and British history. These collections include:

Legal Treatises, 1800-1926: over 20,000 legal treatises provide a comprehensive collection in legal history, business and economics, politics and government.

Trials, 1600-1926: nearly 10,000 titles reveal the drama of famous, infamous, and obscure courtroom cases in America and the British Empire across three centuries.

Primary Sources, 1620-1926: includes reports, statutes and regulations in American history, including early state codes, municipal ordinances, constitutional conventions and compilations, and law dictionaries.

These archives provide a unique research tool for tracking the development of our modern legal system and how it has affected our culture, government, business – nearly every aspect of our everyday life. For the first time, these high-quality digital scans of original works are available via print-on-demand, making them readily accessible to libraries, students, independent scholars, and readers of all ages.

The BiblioLife Network

This project was made possible in part by the BiblioLife Network (BLN), a project aimed at addressing some of the huge challenges facing book preservationists around the world. The BLN includes libraries, library networks, archives, subject matter experts, online communities and library service providers. We believe every book ever published should be available as a high-quality print reproduction; printed on-demand anywhere in the world. This insures the ongoing accessibility of the content and helps generate sustainable revenue for the libraries and organizations that work to preserve these important materials.

The following book is in the "public domain" and represents an authentic reproduction of the text as printed by the original publisher. While we have attempted to accurately maintain the integrity of the original work, there are sometimes problems with the original work or the micro-film from which the books were digitized. This can result in minor errors in reproduction. Possible imperfections include missing and blurred pages, poor pictures, markings and other reproduction issues beyond our control. Because this work is culturally important, we have made it available as part of our commitment to protecting, preserving, and promoting the world's literature.

GUIDE TO FOLD-OUTS MAPS and OVERSIZED IMAGES

The book you are reading was digitized from microfilm captured over the past thirty to forty years. Years after the creation of the original microfilm, the book was converted to digital files and made available in an online database.

In an online database, page images do not need to conform to the size restrictions found in a printed book. When converting these images back into a printed bound book, the page sizes are standardized in ways that maintain the detail of the original. For large images, such as fold-out maps, the original page image is split into two or more pages

Guidelines used to determine how to split the page image follows:

• Some images are split vertically; large images require vertical and horizontal splits.
• For horizontal splits, the content is split left to right.
• For vertical splits, the content is split from top to bottom.
• For both vertical and horizontal splits, the image is processed from top left to bottom right.

THE

LAW OF RENTCHARGES

(COMMONLY CALLED CHIEF RENTS),

MAINLY FROM A CONVEYANCING STANDPOINT.

BY

J. M. EASTON,

OF THE INNER TEMPLE, BARRISTER-AT-LAW, AUTHOR OF "THE LAW AS TO
THE APPOINTMENT OF NEW TRUSTEES," EDITOR OF FOURTH
EDITION "COLLISTER ON COPYRIGHT," COMPILER OF
"THE QUARTERLY NOTES," ETC.

LONDON

STEVENS & HAYNES, 13, BELL YARD, TEMPLE BAR, W.C.

MANCHESTER

MEREDITH, RAY, & LITTLER, 19, KING STREET.

1909

PREFACE.

It does not fall within the province of the writer to enter into a comparison of the merits or demerits of the chief rent system with those of the leasehold system. The main object in either case is to enable a builder to commence operations without having to sink any part of his capital in the purchase of a site, and the determination as to which system shall be adopted will probably depend upon the custom of the particular district in which the land is situate. In certain districts of England—notably in Manchester and its neighbourhood—the custom of selling building land in consideration of a perpetual rentcharge or chief rent—as it is commonly, but erroneously, termed—is firmly established. In such districts the practice is familiar to builders, estate agents, and lawyers, and in spite of the criticisms that are sometimes levelled against the system, it is found, upon the whole, to work smoothly in practice, whilst the chief rents are regarded as sound and desirable investments and consequently find a ready market.

It cannot, however, be denied that the system is one which has given rise to a very special, and often intricate, branch of conveyancing which is not adequately treated in the ordinary text-books on conveyancing. It has been the object of the author to fill this gap. He cannot hope to have covered every point that may arise in practice, but he has endeavoured, to the best of his ability, to consider all those matters which, in his experience, most frequently give rise to difficulty, and many of which are uncovered by direct authority.

The book has not been burdened by including the law of rents as between landlord and tenant, nor has the effect of registration of title been considered. The districts in which the chief rent system prevails all lie outside the compulsory registration area and the author, having had little or no experience of registered titles did not feel himself competent to deal with this aspect of the subject.

One point upon which the author felt considerable hesitation was whether he should include any Forms in the book, and eventually a middle course was decided upon. More or less adequate Forms relating to the creation and transfer of rents are to be found in the standard books of Precedents, and references to most of these have been given in the Appendix, together with a full Form of a Conveyance of several plots of land subject to apportioned parts of a rent—a Form which, it is believed, will be found readily adaptable to varying circumstances.

The Index of Cases gives the dates of the cases cited together with references to all the Reports, including the Revised Reports and the English Reports.

Finally, the Author offers his apologies for a few Addenda and Corrigenda, noted on page xx, due to the fact of his being compelled to correct the proof sheets at a time when he was far from a Law Library.

J. M. EASTON.

40, South King Street,
Manchester,
September, 1909.

TABLE OF CONTENTS.

TABLE OF CASES.

TABLE OF STATUTES.

ADDENDA ET CORRIGENDA.

p 22   Additional authorities for the proposition that the owner of a rentcharge can distrain upon the goods of a lessee unless his lease was prior to the creation of the rent are *Saffery v. Elgood* 1 A. & E. 191 and *Dawson v. Robbins* 2 C. P. D. 38

p 24 n (1)   Add *Hambro v. Hambro* (1894) 2 Ch. 564.

p 24 n (3)   For *Sandeman v. Sandeman* read *Sandeman v. Rushton*

p 41   The reference to *Gallagher v. Naesmith* should be 120 L. T. Journal

THE LAW OF RENTCHARGES.

THE LAW OF RENTCHARGES.

CHAPTER I.

GRANTS OF LAND IN CONSIDERATION OF RENTCHARGES.

ANY person having sufficient estate and being Who may sell on chief. under no disability may sell land in consideration of a rentcharge, and though a rentcharge, as such, cannot continue longer than the estate of the grantor in the land out of which it is to issue, yet it may still continue as a personal annuity[1] or be fed by an estoppel if the grantor subsequently acquires a sufficient estate to satisfy the terms of his grant.[2]

A rentcharge created by a tenant in tail will Tenants in tail only be a charge upon the land during his life, unless he bars the entail.[3]   By sect. 15 of the Fines and Recoveries Act, 1833,[4] every tenant in tail is to have full power to dispose of, for all estates in fee simple or for any less estates, the land entailed as against his own issue and the remaindermen. If, therefore, a tenant in tail conveys to the use that he, the grantor, and his heirs, shall receive a perpetual rent and subject thereto to the use of the grantee in fee simple, the grantee will obtain

---

[1] *Fulwood* v *Ward*, Pop. 87
[2] *Holt* v *Sandbach*, Cro Car

[3] 1 Rep 48
[4] 3 & 4 Will. IV c 74.

103

A

the land, and the grantor will obtain the rent for estates in fee simple, provided the deed be enrolled within six months from the date of its execution.[1]

Tenants for life

In order that a tenant for life may be able to sell in consideration of a perpetual rent he must either have an express power to that effect in his settlement or obtain an order under sect. 10 of the Settled Land Act, 1882.[2] Under this section he can obtain an order authorising a sale in consideration of a rentcharge secured by condition of re-entry or otherwise as the Court directs, upon proof that he is desirous of selling *for building purposes*,[3] and that it is either the custom in the district in which the land is situate to sell upon these terms or difficult to sell on other terms. The rent so created is to go and remain to the uses, on the trusts, and subject to the powers and provisions which immediately before the conveyance were subsisting with respect to the land out of which the rent is reserved.[4]

Trustees and mortgagees

Trustees holding land upon trust for sale or with a power of sale ought generally to sell for a gross sum, and express authority must be conferred by

[1] Ib. s. 40.
45 & 46 Vict. c. 39.
Building purposes include the erecting and the improving of and the adding to and the repairing of buildings, Settled Land Act 1882, sect. 2 sub. s. 10 (iii). See *re Earl of Ellesmere*, W. N. (1898). p. 18. *re Daniell* (1894) 3 Ch. 503.

[2] Settled Land Act 1890 (53 and 54 Vict. c. 69) s. 9. There are various other Statutes enabling tenants for life under particular circumstances to grant rent charges. See Copinger, p. 156 et seq.

the trust instrument before a sale can be effected in consideration of a rent, for otherwise the sale will be invalid,[1] and the same remark would apply to a mortgagee selling under his power of sale. If, however, the trustees held upon trust for sale, and the income of the proceeds were directed to be paid to one for life, the tenant for life might under sect. 63 of the Settled Land Act, 1882, and sect. 7 of the Settled Land Act, 1884,[2] obtain an order permitting him to exercise the powers of a tenant for life under those Acts, and a further order that he be at liberty to sell in consideration of a rentcharge under sect. 10 of the Act of 1882 alluded to above.

The Court of Lunacy can, and will in a proper case where it is proved to be beneficial, authorise the sale in consideration of a rentcharge of land belonging to a lunatic or a person properly detained as such.[3]

Lunatics

A rentcharge is an incorporeal hereditament, and must be created either by deed or will. Where land is sold in consideration of a rent the deed of conveyance may either reserve the rent or the rent may be limited under the Statute of Uses. A reservation was at one time more usual, and the

How rent-charge is created

---

[1] *Read v Shaw*, Sug. Powers 8th Ed pp 864 953 Farwell on Powers, 2nd Ed p 559 but see *re Ware* (1892) 1 Ch 344 347, and Farrer Conditions of Sale 2nd ed 218 where the learned author suggests that in a district where such sales are customary trustees might sell in considera tion of a rent

[2] 47 & 48 Vict c 16

[3] *Re Ware* ubi sup

language of sect. 9 of the Settled Land Act, 1890,[1] seems to imply that this is still the proper method to employ where a tenant for life sells under the powers of the Settled Land Acts. A reservation operates by way of implied grant, and is sometimes followed by an express grant; but, if so, the express grant will be rejected as mere surplusage and the deed will depend upon the implied grant in the reservation.[2] In modern times, however, the practice of reserving a rent has generally yielded to the practice of limiting the rent under the Statute of Uses. The vendor grants to the purchaser and his heirs " to the use " that the vendor and his heirs shall receive the rent and subject thereto to the use of the purchaser and his heirs. The purchaser thereupon being seised to the use of the vendor, the Statute of Uses steps in and executes the use in the vendor, who thus becomes seised of the rent in possession, even prior to his first receipt of rent.[3] If any further use be limited it will be a " use upon a use," and the last use will not be executed by the Statute, but will be an equitable estate only. Thus, if the conveyance be " to the use that X and his heirs shall receive a yearly rent of £5 to the use of Y and his heirs "

---

[1] 53 & 54 Vict. c. 69.

[2] *Hartley* v. *Maddocks* (1899) 2 Ch. 199. Where a rent is reserved the deed ought properly to be executed by both grantor and grantee; but if the grantee omit to do so the rent will not withstanding be well created in equity; for whoever claims an estate under a deed is in equity obliged to fulfil all the terms of the deed. Gilbert Rents 16, 17.

[3] *Hodges* v. *Blain* 18 C. B. N. S. 90. *Orme's Case* L. R. 8 C. P. 281.

the legal estate in the rent will be in X, and Y will only have an equitable estate.[1] Moreover, if the sale be to a corporation—including, of course, a company incorporated under the Companies' Act—it will be essential to insert in the conveyance a grantee to uses, for the Statute of Uses only operates " where any *person or persons* . . . shall stand or be seised of and in any . . . hereditaments," &c., and consequently a corporation cannot be seised to a use [2] The grant should therefore run " to X and his heirs to the use that the vendor and his heirs shall receive a yearly rent of £x and subject thereto to the use of the corporation." On the other hand, there is no necessity for a grantee to uses in the case of a sale by a corporation to a private individual in consideration of a rent, because the Statute of Uses does apply when any person is seised " to the use, confidence or trust of any other person or persons *or of any body politic.*"

A rentcharge may be limited for any estate which could be created in the land out of which it issues, that is to say, for life, in tail,[3] in fee simple, or for years But if the rent is to endure for longer than the grantee's life proper words of limitation

Estates that may be created in rents

---

[1] *Chaplin v Chaplin* 3 P. Wms 229 231 Co Litt 298a

[2] See Challis R P p 354 2nd ed

[3] Note, however that if a rent be granted " to X and the heirs of his body " without any remainder in fee X cannot by barring the entail obtain a rent in fee but a base fee only, for otherwise the burden upon the inheritance would be increased (Co Litt 298 a)

must be inserted in the grant—that is to say, both in the limitation of the estate of the grantee to uses and that of the rentowner. Thus, a grant " to A to the use that B and his heirs shall receive a rent of £x " confers upon B a rent during A's life only, for it is essential that a use shall be supported by sufficient seisin, and A has under this form of grant only a life estate. Again, if the grant be " to A and his heirs to the use that B shall receive a rent of £x." B only has a rent during his own life. The only proper words for limiting a rent in fee are to B " and his heirs "—or to B " in fee simple " in deeds executed since the Conveyancing Act, 1881.[1]

How rents created under powers contained in settlements should be limited

Words of limitation may, however, be incorporated by reference to another document,[2] and therefore the not infrequent method, where a tenant for life sells in consideration of a rentcharge under a power in the settlement of limiting the rent " to the vendor or other the person or persons who would for the time being under the settlement have been entitled to the hereditaments hereby granted if these presents had not been made " is probably effectual. It has, however, been suggested[3] that if land be limited to the use that one shall receive a rent during his life and after his death to the use that his first and other sons successively and the heirs of their respective bodies

[1] 44 & 45 Vict c 41 sect 51
See re Ethel & Butler (1901) 1
Ch 945 Dist re Lord & Fergusson (1906) 1 Ir Rep 607

[2] Co Litt 9 b Gardr v
Gardr 3 Dr & War 13

[3] Co Litt Supp 271 b n
(1) Lewis on Perpetuities p 612

shall receive the rent, these are distinct rents, and consequently the rent to the second son is too remote, being limited to take effect after an indefinite failure of issue of the first son. It is therefore considered to be the safer course where a rent is to be limited to the uses of a settlement to limit it to the tenant for life "and his heirs" or other the person or persons, &c.,[1] so as to first limit the rent as a whole and carve out of it the lesser estates.[2]

If, however, the land be sold by a tenant for life in consideration of a rent under sect. 10 of the Settled Land Act, 1882, this difficulty appears to be avoided by sect. 9 of the Settled Land Act, 1890, which provides that where land is expressed to be conveyed in fee simple with a reservation of a "perpetual rent or rentcharge"[3] the reservation is to operate to create a rentcharge in fee simple, and so that the rentcharge is to go and remain to the uses on the trusts and subject to the powers and provisions which immediately before the conveyance were subsisting with respect to the land out of which it is reserved.

A conveyance of land to tenants in common reserving to the vendor a rent will only operate to confer on the vendor a single rent, for the deed

---

[1] See 2 Davidson Pt. I. p. 571 Copinger p 672

[2] *Hedges v. Peach* Salk. 577

[3] *i.e. Semble* without the necessity for any words of limitation whatsoever

will be construed most strongly against the grantor.[1]

If A and B, tenants in common, desire to sell in consideration of a rentcharge, the most satisfactory course is to create distinct rents to A and B, giving to each powers of distress and entry over specified portions of the land conveyed. But if this cannot be arranged it will probably still be the better course to create distinct rents, so that each co-owner may have a separate covenant for the payment of his rent. There would appear to be little objection to giving to each a power of distress over the entirety of the land,[2] but there is greater difficulty as to the proper form of the powers of entry, if any. This point will, however, be reserved until after a consideration of the usual remedies conferred upon a rentowner for the recovery of his rent.

A rent may be limited so as to commence at a future date, provided the commencement is within the perpetuity period,[3] for a rent created *de novo* lies in grant and not in seisin, and consequently is not dependent upon the common law rules as to seisin.[4]

The following are the remedies conferred upon a

[1] Co. Litt. 197 a. It is otherwise in the case of a grant of a rent by tenants in common *ib* sec Post Chapter v

[2] Cf. *Rivis v. Watson* 5 M. & W. 255 *Whitlock v. Roberts*, M.& Y. 107

[3] Plowd. 156 Lewis on Perpetuities 642 Gray on Perp sects 16 17

[4] It is otherwise as to conveyances of rents already in existence see Post Chap. iv

rentowner for the recovery of his rent which are most usually to be met with : (1) The landowner's covenant to pay, (2) a power of distress, (3) a power of entry and perception of rents and profits until thereout the rentowner be satisfied of the arrears of his rent and costs and expenses, (4) a power to mortgage or lease for the purpose of raising such arrears, costs, and expenses,[1] and (5) a power of absolute re-entry.

The agreement between the vendor and pur-chaser ought always to state which of these remedies are to be inserted, and the wording of sect. 10 of the Settled Land Act, 1882, seems to imply that an order obtained by a tenant for life authorising him to sell in consideration of a rentcharge ought to expressly state the remedies to be given for the recovery of the rent.[2] Subject to any express stipulation in the agreement the vendor is entitled to insert a power of distress and a covenant to pay[3], but it is doubtful whether he is entitled to insert a power of entry for perception of rents and profits.[4] A provision, however, in the agreement that " all proper powers " are to be inserted will justify the

[1] This power was only usual in the case of jointure rent charges and the like, but it has been extended to all rentcharges by sect. 44 of the Conveyancing Act 1881.

[2] The order will generally direct that sales are to be made on the conditions made appli-cable to leases by sects 7 & 8 of the Act with any necessary modifications.

[3] *Bower v. Cooper* 2 Ha 408

[4] *Hassel v. Gowthwaite* Willes 500 but see *Foster v. Foster,* 2 Vern 386 as to implication of such a power

insertion in the conveyance of such last-mentioned power, but, *semble*, not a power of absolute re-entry.[1]

Personal liability of terre tenant

Even if there is no express covenant by the land-owner for payment of the rent he will be liable in debt to the rentowner,[2] but this liability only extends to instalments falling due during the occupation of the landowner, and by conveying the land to another he can escape liability in respect of future instalments. A person, however, who has expressly covenanted to pay the rent remains liable for the rest of his life, and even after death there would appear to be no way of clearing his estate of its contingent liability except by his representatives distributing his estate under the direction of the Court.[3]

Remedies may be given by means of common law condition or springing use

The remedies for recovery of the rent may either be set out at length in the conveyance or reliance may be placed upon sect. 44 of the Conveyancing and Law of Property Act, 1881, which impliedly confers upon the owner of a rentcharge certain

---

[1] *Ex Parte Ralph* 1 De Gex 219

[2] See post Chapter II where this subject is more fully considered

[3] It is true that there is a curious section (sect. 28) of Lord St Leonard's Act 1859 (22 & 23 Vict c 35) to the effect that an executor or administrator having satisfied all present liabilities *and conveyed the land subject to the rent to a purchaser* and distributed the estate is to cease to be personally liable in respect of the rent but inasmuch as prior to the Land Transfer Act 1897 (60 & 61 Vict c 65) an executor could rarely convey a freehold estate in land since it did not vest in him this would appear to have been a particularly fatuous piece of legislation Has the Land Transfer Act enlarged the scope of the former Act? See *Millar v Sinclair* (1903) 1 Ir R 150

remedies for its recovery. If the powers be set out at length, they may be granted either by way of springing use or by proviso, *i.e.*, by a common law condition. In practice it is more usual to adopt the expedient of the springing use—thus, the vendor grants the land to the purchaser and his heirs to the use that the vendor and his heirs may receive the rent, and to the further use that if the rent shall be in arrear for over a certain fixed time it shall be lawful for the vendor, his heirs, or assigns, to enter and distrain, and so forth. As soon as the rent becomes in arrear beyond the fixed period a use springs up and vests in the vendor, being immediately transferred into possession by the operation of the Statute of Uses. As soon, again, as the rent in arrear is satisfied, the use and possession will determine until the recurrence of the event upon the happening of which they are to arise.

The objection to inserting a common law condition of re-entry formerly was that the benefit of such a condition could only be reserved to the grantor and his heirs, and was not assignable unless it passed as incident to the estate in the rent[1] which it has been held a power of entry for perception of rents and profits does[2]. It is now provided by sect. 6 of the Real Property Amendment Act, 1845,[3] that all rights of entry both present and

---

[1] Co. Litt. 201, 214, 215 ; Shep. Touch. 120
[2] *Havergill v. Hare* Cro. Jac. 510
[3] 8 & 9 Vict. c. 106

future may be assigned, but it has been said that this section applies only where a party has a right to recover his land, and his right of entry, and nothing but that, remains, and does not extend to a right of entry after the condition has been broken.[1]

The remedies conferred by the Conveyancing Act 1881 — Three of the usual remedies above referred to are conferred upon the owners of rentcharges by sect. 44 of the Conveyancing Act, 1881,[2] viz.: (1) A power if at any time the rent or any part thereof is unpaid for *twenty-one* days next after the time appointed for any payment in respect thereof for the person entitled to receive the rent to enter into and distrain on the land charged or any part thereof and dispose according to law of any distress found, to the intent that thereby or otherwise the rent and all arrears thereof, and all costs and expenses occasioned by non-payment thereof, may be fully paid. (2) A power if at any time the rent or any part thereof is unpaid for *forty* days next after the time appointed for any payment in respect thereof, although no legal demand has been made for payment thereof, for the person entitled to receive the rent to enter into possession of and hold the land charged or any part thereof, and take the income thereof until thereby or otherwise the rent and all arrears thereof due at the time of his entry or becoming due during his continuance in

---

[1] Per Pollock C. B. *Hunt v. Jenkins v. Jones* 9 Q. B. D. 131
Bishop 8 Ex. 680. *Hunt v. Challis R. P. 2nd ed. p. 167
Remnant* 9 Ex. 640. But see   [2] 44 & 45 Vict. c. 41

possession, and all costs and expenses occasioned by non-payment of the rent are fully paid, such possession, when taken, to be without impeachment of waste: (3) a power in the like case for the person entitled to the rent, whether taking possession or not, by deed to demise the land charged, or any part thereof, to a trustee for a term of years with or without impeachment of waste, on trust by mortgage, or sale, or demise, for all or any part of the term, of the land charged or any part thereof, or by receipt of the income thereof, or by all or any of those means, or by any other reasonable means, to raise and pay the rent and all arrears thereof due or to become due, and all costs and expenses occasioned by non-payment of the rent or incurred in compelling or obtaining payment thereof, or otherwise relating thereto, including the costs of the preparation and execution of the deed of demise and the costs of the execution of the trusts of that deed: the surplus, if any, of the money raised or the income received under the trusts of that deed to be paid to the person for the time being entitled to the land therein comprised in reversion immediately expectant upon the term thereby created

These provisions follow closely the forms of remedies that have been usually set out at length in deeds creating rents, except that it has not been usual to insert a power of leasing in grants of rents in fee. The section, however, confers no absolute power of re-entry, however long the rent may be in arrear

Chap I. and it is still necessary to insert such a power in the deed, if required.

Sect 44 does not apply to instruments before 1882, or where contrary intention expressed
The section, too, applies only where the instrument under which the rent arises comes into operation after the 31st December, 1881,[1] and does not express a contrary intention.[2] It has been suggested[3] that a rentcharge created under a power to limit a rent might be held to date from the creation of the power and not from the date of its exercise, so that if the instrument giving the power was dated before the year 1882 it may be well to insert the remedies expressly and not rely upon the section under consideration : but it is thought that no such doubt can exist where the power is not to limit a rent directly, but to sell the land in consideration of a rent. It is also thought that if the instrument creating the rent expressly includes some of the powers given by sect. 44 this is not such an expression of a contrary intention as to necessarily exclude the other powers.[1]

Whether the usual remedies infringe the rule against perpetuities
There is another limitation to the operation of the section, and that is that the powers thereby conferred are to be effectual "so far as those remedies might have been conferred by the instrument under which the rent arises, but not further."

---

[1] Sub section (6) A clause of distress was, however, implied by the 4 Geo II c 28 sect 5

[2] Sub sec (5)

[3] Hood & Challis p 135 (7th ed)

[4] *Searle* v *Cook* 43 Ch D 519 533 and cf *Cecil* v *Langdon* 28 Ch D 1 *Life Interest Corporation* v *Hand in Hand Society* (1898) 2 Ch 230 re *Burke* (1908) 2 Ch 248

Sect 44 sub sect (1)

and this leads to a consideration of how far these powers and the powers which it has hitherto been the practice to insert in deeds creating rentcharges for securing the rentcharge, are valid.

In modern times these powers have been the subject of attack, but it is believed that no suggestion has yet been made or could properly be made that a general power of distress is invalid,[1] but it has frequently been contended that powers of entry for perception of rents and profits, powers of absolute re-entry, and powers of limiting terms are all void unless they are limited to arise within the period of perpetuity. A considerable amount of confusion prevails with reference to these matters, and it is necessary to distinguish (1) powers of re-entry for breach of a covenant from powers of re-entry for non-payment of the rent (2) powers of entry for perception of rents and profits until arrears be satisfied from powers of absolute re-entry; (3) powers to limit terms to endure only so long as the rentowner has possession from powers to limit absolute terms and, possibly, (4) powers of entry arising under the Statute of

[1] Williams V. & P. p 597 It must be understood that we are here speaking of a power of distress over land which is subject to a rent for the purpose of securing the rent itself The validity of powers of distress for the purpose of indemnity against an over riding rent will be discussed later See Chapter III post p 45

Uses from powers arising under common law conditions.[1]

With regard to powers of re-entry for breach of covenant it is clear that these are void unless confined to the perpetuity period. They are not given for the purpose of securing the rent, except in an indirect manner, and their invalidity has been determined by the case of *Dunn* v. *Flood*.[2] But as to the validity or invalidity of powers of entry for non-payment of the rent there is, it is believed, a total absence of any modern authority, for the case of *Dunn* v. *Flood*[3], which is sometimes quoted as a decision against their validity was not a case of entry for non-payment of rent, but for breach of a covenant. The majority of modern text-book writers consider that a power of entry for perception of rents and profits need not be,[4] but that a power of absolute re-entry ought to be,[5] confined to the perpetuity period. The distinction between

1 Mr Williams in his work on Vendors and Purchasers, contends that it is still open to argument that common law conditions do not fall within the rule against perpetuities, in spite of the decision *in re Hollis' Hospital* (1899) 2 Ch 540. See *Switzer* v. *Rochford* (1906) 1 Ir R 399. *Att.-Gen* v. *Cummins* (1906), 1 Ir R 406

2 25 Ch D 629 on app 28 Ch D 586. See also *London and S W Ry* v. *Gomm.* 20 Ch D 562 *re Hollis' Hospital* (1899), 2 Ch 540

3 Ub sup

4 Copinger 64. Lewis on Perp 618. Williams V & P 507. 12 Enc of Prec 213. Wolstenholme's Conveyancing Acts 9th ed, 112. Contra 1 K & E 338

5 Williams V & P 509. 12 Enc of Prec 213. Gray on Perp sect 303. Contra Copinger 68. Lewis on Perp 618. and see an Article 17 Law Quarterly p 32. In America absolute powers of re entry in perpetuity have been upheld. Gray on Perp sect 309

a power of entry for non-payment of the rent and a similar power on breach of a covenant lies in the fact that the object of the former power is to secure the rent itself, in which the rentowner has a " present estate and which passes as incident to the rent ;"[1] whilst the latter power may have other objects. The distinction between a power of entry for perception of rents and profits and a power of absolute re-entry lies in the fact that in case of exercise of the former power the estate in the land is no greater than the estate in the rent, and the possession of the rentowner can always be determined by payment of the arrears of rent and costs ; whilst if the latter power is exercised, the land is to be forfeited, although its value may be more than sufficient to pay the rent.

The case of *Havergill* v. *Hare*[2] might perhaps be cited as an authority for the validity of unrestricted powers of entry for perception of rents and profits —at least no question of perpetuity appears to have been raised ; but against this it may be said that the case was decided prior to the modern developments of the rule against perpetuities. The same remark applies to the passage in Gilbert on Rents,[3] which treats such powers of entry as unquestionably valid, and appears to draw no distinction between a power of entry for perception of rents and profits and a power of absolute re-entry. It

[1] *Havergill* v *Hare*, Cro Jac 510.

[2] Ub sup See also *Doe* v *Bateman*, 2 B & Ald. 168, 170

[3] pp 135 et seq

may indeed be contended with some show of plausibility that there is no solid distinction in principle between the two powers, and that the object of both is to secure the rent[1]: that the power of absolute re-entry is only likely to be brought into operation in a case where the property upon which the rent is charged is an insufficient security for the rent, in which case entry for perception of rents and profits would practically be equivalent to absolute re-entry, and that an absolute re-entry is such a penalty as would be always relieved against in a Court of Equity[2] But the answer to this form of argument is that, in applying the rule against perpetuities, regard must be had to possible events, and the remedy by absolute re-entry is not necessarily co-extensive with the breach it is sought to remedy, and it is submitted that—unless another exception to the rule against perpetuities is to be admitted, grounded upon the long-standing practice of conveyancers—powers of absolute re-entry, but not powers of entry for perception of rents and

---

[1] Merely remedial powers perhaps do not fall within the rule against perpetuities Gray on Perp sects 273a, 303, 316, 329

[2] Co Litt 203 a 3 Cruise Dig 286 Speaking of relief against forfeiture of estates Lord Macclesfield states that the true ground of relief against penalties is from the original intent of the case where the penalty is designed only to secure money and the Court gives him all that he expected or desired *Peachy* v *Duke of Somerset* 1 Stra 447 2 W & T L C Eq 250 (7th ed) Courts of Equity relieved a lessee from forfeiture for non payment of his rent long before the principle was recognized by the Legislature

profits, should preferably be confined to the perpetuity period.

But the draughtsman who simply confines his powers to the perpetuity period is possibly laying up trouble for a future generation, and it is submitted that he ought, confining the powers to entry for non-payment of the rent and not for breach of the covenant to pay, to make them exercisable during the perpetuity period, 'or such further period as may not be contrary to the law against perpetuities.' It must be remembered that unlimited powers both of entry for perception of rents and profits and of absolute re-entry have frequently been enforced without the landowners having had the temerity to question their validity.

The power to limit a term appears to stand or fall with the powers of entry. In *Havergill* v. *Hare*[1] it was held that the owner of a rent having a power of entry for perception of rents and profits might create a term to endure so long as he remained in possession but a power to limit an absolute term must, it is considered, be void if a power of absolute re-entry is void. It is, therefore, safer to confine the power given by sub-sect. 4 of sect. 44 of the Conveyancing Act, or any similar express power, to the perpetuity period or such further period as may not be contrary to law.[2]

[1] Cro Jac 510

[2] A Conveyancing Bill now before Parliament proposes to free the statutory powers conferred by sect 44 from all doubts as to their infringing the perpetuity rule

It would seem, however, to follow from the wording of sect. 9 of the Settled Land Act, 1890,[1] that the powers and remedies conferred by sect. 44 of the Conveyancing Act are valid, although possibly infringing the perpetuity period, in a case where a rent has been created by a tenant for life under the powers of the Settled Land Acts.

The draughtsman should be careful to see that in limiting express powers for recovery of the rent they are as large as the estate in the rent. If the rent be created in fee the powers of distress and entry should be given to the rentowner, "his heirs and assigns," for if the rent be given to " A and his heirs," but the powers of distress to A only, this will be a good grant of a rentcharge during the life of A, but a rent *seck* as regards his heirs.[2]

Where the rent is reserved to tenants in common, or joint tenants, it must be made clear by whom the remedies for non-payment of the rent are to be exercised. If the powers of distress and entry are given simply to two joint tenants or two tenants in common, neither could enforce the remedies without the other,[3] and it is therefore usual to limit the powers to the two, " or either of them." Each could then distrain for his share of rent in arrear, or, if both shares were in arrear, they might

---

1 53 & 54 Vict c 69

2 Gilbert 46 Copinger. 53

3 *Humphrey* v *Stenbury* (1909) 1 Ch 244 And if a rent held in severalty descends to two as coparceners *semble* the powers of entry cannot be exercised by one without the other *Doe* v *Lewis* 5 A & E 277

join in making the distress.[1] If the power of
entry and perception of rents and profits be given to
tenants in common "or either of them," as suggested,
it is submitted that either could receive the whole of
the rents, until notice were given to the lessees by
the owner of the other moiety of the rent,[2] and that
if one tenant in common exercised his power of
absolute re-entry without the other, the former
would become tenant in common of the land with
the terre tenant, subject to the other moiety of
the rent. This might operate to the prejudice of
the entering rentowner, and it may perhaps be
advisable to give power to each tenant in common
if his share of rent is in arrear and his co-tenant
will not join with him, to re-enter upon the entirety
and hold the same in trust for himself and his
co-tenant.

The primary remedy for the recovery of the rent
is the power of distress. The law of distress as
between landlord and tenant has been profoundly
altered by the recent Law of Distress Amendment
Act, 1909,[3] which, in effect, exempts the goods of a
stranger from distress for rent and renders a sub-
lessee at a rack-rent exempt upon payment to the
distraining landlord of the rent due to his immediate
lessor.[4] This Act, however, only applies as between
landlord and tenant, and makes no alteration in

The power of distress.

---

[1] Litt. sect. 317 *Puller v Palmer* 3 Salk 207. *Whitley v Roberts,* 1 Mc'Lel. & Y 107 Bullen on Distress, p 50 (2nd ed.)

[2] *Harrison v Barnby,* 5 T R 246

[3] 8 Edw VII c 53.

[4] Sect 1

the law as to distress by the owner of a rentcharge, who, if his rent be in arrear, may distrain upon the goods of either a stranger or a lessee, unless the latter's lease were granted before the creation of the rentcharge.[1] It has, however, been the frequent practice in giving express powers of distress for the recovery of a rentcharge to state that the power to distrain is to be " as landlords may distrain for rent reserved upon a lease" It will be well in future to omit these words, having regard to the provisions of the above-mentioned Act.

Where the land out of which the rent issues has been let at a rack-rent it will generally be considered inadvisable, if the rent is in arrear, to distrain upon the tenant, and the power of entry for perception of rents and profits will be useful in such a case; but it would seem that the rentowner cannot recover the cost of repairs done by him during the period he is in possession,[2] nor must he injure the inheritance.[3] Moreover, the power of entry for

---

[1] *Re Herbage Rents Greenwich* (1896). 2 Ch 811 815 816. but if the tenant pays under threat of distress possibly he may deduct the payment from his rent *Taylor* v *Zamira* 6 Taunt 524

[2] *Hooper* v *Cooke* 25 L J Ch 62 467 20 Beav 639

[3] *Doe* v *Horsley* 1 A & E 766 *Doe* v *Bowditch* 8 Q B 973 unless *semble* he is expressly made unimpeachable for waste

It would seem that a rent owner in possession under a power of entry for perception of rents and profits might enforce the covenants in leases granted by the terre tenant that power being given by sect 10 of the Conveyancing Act 1881 (44 and 45 Vict c 41) to " the person entitled subject to the term to the income of the whole or any part of the land leased " See *Turner* v *Walsh* (1909) 2 K B 484

perception of rents and profits does not empower the receipt of rent reserved upon a lease created prior to the grant of the rentcharge, and in such a case the power of granting leases may be employed, the new lease being, of course, created for a longer term than the original lease so as to create a fresh reversion. This power of granting leases may also be useful where the land subject to the rentcharge is vacant, though in such a case the rentowner will probably exercise his power of absolute re-entry, if such is given him by the instrument creating the rent.

The rentowner cannot forfeit for non-payment For of rent until he has legally demanded his rent, *i.e.*, forfeiture has demanded upon the land the precise amount on the exact day it is due, unless, as is usually the case, the deed dispenses with the necessity for a legal demand.[1] Upon re-entering the rentowner can avoid all mesne charges and incumbrances.[2] The issue of an unequivocal writ demanding possession is equivalent to an actual entry.[3]

After the powers and remedies for the recovery Sale by of the rent the deed creating the rent will limit the Court land "subject to and charged with" the rent to the use of the purchaser in fee simple. Even, however, in the absence of such words the land will be charged with the rent, and the rentowner, if the rent be in arrear, may apply to the Court for an

---

[1] 1 Wm Saunders 286 b, n (16). As to relief see ante p

[2] Co Litt 202

[3] *Moore v Ullcoats Mining Company* (1908) 1 Ch 575

order for the sale of sufficient part of the land to raise the arrears,[1] but the grant of such an order is discretionary and cannot be claimed as of right.[2]

Building and other covenants and the remedies for breaches thereof

Then follow the covenants. The first covenant will be for payment of the rent. The covenants relating to the erection, maintenance, and repair of the buildings are of importance to the rentowner as affecting the security for his rent, particularly as it has been held that, in the absence of agreement, a rentowner has no equity to prevent the terre tenant from committing waste.[3] It must, however, be remembered that it is now firmly established that the burden of covenants only runs with the land in the strict sense, i.e., so as to found an action at law for breach, as between landlord and tenant, though, in equity, a purchaser of freeholds will be bound by restrictive, but not positive, covenants entered into by his predecessor in title of which the purchaser has notice, express or constructive, at the date of his purchase.[4] The personal liability upon the

---

[1] *Cupit* v *Jackson* McClel 495 *Pettinger* v *Ambler* 24 Beav 542 *White* v *James* 26 ib 191 *Todd* v *Bielby* 27 ib 353 *Taylor* v *Taylor*, 17 Eq 321 *Horton* v *Hall*, ib 437 *Scottish Widows' Fund* v *Craig*, 20 Ch D 208

[2] *Hall* v *Hart*, 2 J & H 76 *Tucker* v *Tucker* (1893), 2 Ch 323 *Blackburne* v *Hope Edwards* (1901) 1 Ch 419

[3] *Sandeman* v *Sandeman*, 61 L J Ch 186 It is nevertheless submitted that in spite of this decision, a terre tenant who wilfully demolished buildings and thereby jeopardised the security for the rent would be restrained by injunction

[4] *Tulk* v *Moxhay* 2 Ph 774 *Haywood* v *Brunswick Building Society* 8 Q B D 403 *Rogers* v *Hosegood* (1900) 2 Ch 388 *re Nisbet and Potts* (1905), 1 Ch. 391 (1906) 1 Ch 386

covenants is therefore precarious, and it is always advisable, if possible, to give the rent-owner other remedies for their enforcement. This is a matter to which sufficient attention is not always given. Care is, indeed, taken to secure that the buildings be actually erected, either by postponing conveyance until they are completed, or by giving a power of absolute re-entry if they are not finished within a definite time ; but the same attention is not always paid to the repairing covenants, although the selling value of a rentcharge will probably be impaired if the buildings upon which it is secured are in a bad state of repair, even though the rent may have been regularly paid It is not unusual to find that an absolute power of re-entry is given only when the property has been out of repair for two years, but this is too long a period to suffer the decay, and it is better either to make the period for forfeiture a shorter one or to empower the rentowner to enter and himself do the repairs, charging the costs upon the inheritance Occasionally a fresh rent is limited by way of indemnity against a breach of any of the covenants.

All powers of entry for breach of the building and other covenants must, as previously pointed out,[1] be confined to the perpetuity period, and prior to enforcing an absolute power of re-entry for breach of covenant, the rentowner must serve the terre tenant with a written notice requiring him to repair

[1] Ante p 16

the breaches of covenant that have occurred.[1] The rentowner will be entitled to the costs of his notice, but not, apparently, to his surveyor's or solicitor's costs of preparing the notice.[2] Sect. 2 of the Conveyancing Act, 1892,[3] which was passed in order to remedy this injustice, seems to be confined to the case where the relationship of landlord and tenant exists.[4]

Powers to redeem the rent

Occasionally there is inserted in the conveyance a power for the purchaser to redeem the rent at a fixed price. Such an option would, it is submitted, be void if exerciseable beyond the perpetuity period.[5]

Who prepares the conveyance.

Where land is sold in consideration of a rentcharge the agreement ought always to provide by whom the conveyance is to be prepared. In the absence of any special provision Part II. of Schedule I. of the General Order under the Solicitors' Remuneration Act, 1881,[6] seems to be framed on the assumption that the vendor prepares the conveyance at the purchaser's expense following the

---

[1] Conveyancing Act, 1881 (44 and 45 Vict. c. 41) sect. 14 sub sect. (3). If the term tenant cannot be found see sect. 67 of the same Act. It is sometimes considered advisable to insert a clause expressly to the effect that notice shall be given to any mortgagees of whose mortgages the rentowner has been given notice.

[2] *Skinners Co. v. Knight* (1891) 2 Q.B. 542.

[3] 55 & 56 Vict. c. 13.

[4] *Rand v. Nineteenth Century Building Society* (1894) 2 Q.B. 226.

L. & S.W. Ry. v. Gomm, 20 Ch.D. 562. *Woodall v. Clifton* (1905) 2 Ch. 257. But see *Switzer v. Rochford* (1906) 1 Ir. Rep. 399 and cf. *Mayor of Worthing v. Heather* (1906), 2 Ch. 532.

[6] 44 & 45 Vict. c. 44.

practice in the case of grants of leases; but it was stated in an opinion given by the Incorporated Law Society in the year 1887 that, in the absence of a custom to the contrary, the conveyance ought always to be prepared by the purchaser.[1] The purchaser ought at his own expense to furnish the vendor with a duplicate conveyance properly stamped.

The title deeds are usually retained by the vendor, even where they only relate to the property sold. This practice may possibly be difficult to defend,[2] but the fact that the title deeds are as necessary to the vendor to prove his title to the rent as to the purchaser to prove his title to the land, may perhaps justify the practice.[3] If, however, the deeds are retained by the vendor, he should give an acknowledgment of the purchaser's right to production and a memorandum of the present deed should be indorsed on the deed of conveyance vesting the property in the vendor

---

[1] Practice and Usage Opinions 1898 p 43 It is thought that in Manchester and several other places there is a custom to the contrary In December 1898 however the Manchester Incorporated Law Society passed the following resolution 'That in the absence of any express stipulation to the contrary where land is conveyed for a bona fide consideration *and* a chief rent is made payable the solicitor for the purchaser is entitled to prepare the conveyance without regard to the amount of consideration paid down and in the opinion of this committee the purchaser should at his own expense furnish a duplicate or counterpart to the vendor duly stamped

[2] *Whitfield v Faussett* 1 Ves Sen 394 *Hooper v Cooke* 20 Beav at p 644

[3] Cf *re Lehmann & Walker* (1906) 2 Ch 640

Chap. 1. or the person from whom he derived his title:
because when a person is allowed to hold a deed
which makes him the ostensible owner of a larger
estate than, according to the existing facts, belongs
to him, it is always proper to indorse upon the
deed some notice of the subsequent transactions
which have curtailed or qualified his estate, in
order to preclude the possibility of any improper
use being made of the deed.

Stamp duty   The conveyance must bear an *ad valorem* stamp
upon twenty times the annual value of the rent
reserved,[1] and if the conveyance be by a mortgagor
and mortgagee and the security is shifted from the
land to the rent, additional *ad valorem* duty will
have to be paid in respect of the substituted
security, limited, however, to ten shillings.[2]

Sale by mortga gor and mortga-gee in con-sideration of a rent as substi-tuted security   Where a mortgagor and mortgagee join in selling
in consideration of a rentcharge which is to be
taken as a substituted security, the rent will be
limited to the use of the mortgagee and his heirs,
and the deed will contain a proviso that the rent
shall be subject to the like equity of redemption
and powers as the land conveyed was subject prior
to the execution of that conveyance, but that, until
notice is given by the mortgagee requiring payment of the rent to him, the rent shall be paid to
the mortgagor, whose receipt shall be a good discharge for the rent   The legal estate, how-

[1] Stamp Act 1891 (54 & 55
Vict c 39), sect 56

[2] Alpe on Stamp Duties, p
114 (11th ed)

ever, in the rent will be in the mortgagee, and any proceedings necessary for its recovery will have to be taken in his name. To avoid this difficulty an agreement on the part of the mortgagee is sometimes inserted in the conveyance providing that he will, at any time before notice has been given by him requiring payment of the rent to himself, at the cost of the mortgagor execute such power of attorney as may be necessary to enable the latter to sue for and recover the rent.

CHAPTER II.

CONVEYANCE OF AN ENTIRE PLOT OF LAND SUBJECT TO A RENTCHARGE.

Liability
of land
does not
depend
on notice

A PURCHASER of land which is subject to a legal rentcharge will, of course, hold subject to the rent, even though he had no notice of the existence of the rent at the time of his purchase.

Vendor
must
disclose
existence
of rents

It is the duty of a vendor, prior to entering into the contract, to disclose the existence of all rents to which the property to be sold is subject. No sufficient disclosure is made by a mere statement in the particulars of sale that the property is sold " subject to all chief rents," and the vendor will, notwithstanding, be unable to force the purchaser to complete his purchase, although if the vendor has been honest he may be entitled to rescind the contract under the usual rescission clause, without making any compensation to the purchaser beyond the return of his deposit.[1] If the rent were small or were secured upon other property besides that contracted to be sold the case might be one for compensation and not rescission.[2]

[1] Re Simpson & Moy, 53 Sol J 376

[2] Hone v Oakstatter 53 Sol J 286 L dale v Stephenson 1 Sim & St 122 Halsey v Grant 13 Ves 73 Horniblow v Shir ley 13 Ves 81 As to the basis of compensation see Powell v South Wales Ry Co 1 Jur N S 773 where the vendor was ordered to give a personal in demnity in addition to com pensation

Moreover, a contract to sell a "freehold" means an unincumbered freehold, and if the property be subject to restrictive covenants the existence of which has not been disclosed the purchaser will be entitled to the return of his deposit and to cancel the contract.[1] A not infrequent practice, where land which is subject to restrictive covenants is to be sold by auction, is to state in the particulars of sale that the property is sold subject to restrictions contained in a certain deed. An offer is made to produce the deed, either at or prior to the sale, and a condition of sale is inserted to the effect that the purchaser shall be deemed to have notice of the terms of the deed whether he inspects it or not. No doubt such a condition is effectual if reasonable opportunity for inspection is afforded, but if the restrictive covenants are of an unusual character further opportunity for inspecting the covenants ought to be afforded than by production of the deed at the time of the auction.[2]

If the property is subject to an over-riding rent, this, too, ought to be stated in the particulars of sale, even where the property to be sold has been indemnified against the over-riding rent. It not infrequently happens that a vendor has not got the possession of the deed conferring the indemnity against the over-riding rent, and is perhaps un-

[1] *Hone v Gakstatter* 53 Sol J 286 *Flight v Booth* 1 Bing 370

[2] *Dougherty v Oates* 45 Sol J 119 *Haedicke v Lipski* (1901) 2 Ch 666 *Molyneux v Hawtrey* (1903) 2 K B 487

Chap II. able to state precisely what form the indemnity takes.[1]   In such case—and in any case where the indemnities are doubtful—a special condition will be necessary providing that the purchaser shall be satisfied with such indemnities (if any) as may appear from the abstract to exist, and that he shall assume, unless he can prove the contrary, that the over-riding rent has been paid down to the date of completion

Indemnities against over riding rents should be expressly assigned. It is always advisable when land which is indemnified against an over-riding rent is conveyed, to expressly assign the benefit of all indemnities, for it is not clear that such indemnities will run with the indemnified land[2] in the absence of express assignment.[3]

Last receipt for rent to be evidence of performance of covenants. Upon the sale of a lease the production of the receipt for the last payment due for rent is prima facie evidence that the covenants in the lease have been performed up to the date of completion,[1] but there is no similar provision that production of the receipt for the last payment due for a rent-charge shall be evidence of the performance of the covenants in the deed creating the rentcharge.

---

[1] The various forms of indemnity usual in practice will be found to be considered in Chapter III If in the contract of sale the property sold is stated to be "indemnified" against a rent, this means a proper and effective indemnity *Manifold v. Johnston* (1902), 1 Ir. R. 7.

[2] Moore 179 *Cook v. Arundel,* Hard 87 1 Eq Ca Ab 26

[3] *Allerton v. Eden,* Noy 5; 2 And 126 pl 72

[1] Conveyancing Act 1881 (44 and 45 Vict c 41), s 3 (1)

It is therefore usual to insert a condition of sale to this effect.

If the land subject to the rent is to be sold in consideration of a gross sum the conveyance will be prepared in the ordinary way by the purchaser's solicitor. The conveyance will be expressed to be " subject to " the rent, and such words will impose upon the purchaser an equitable obligation to indemnify the vendor against future payments of the rent.[1] But the vendor, if he will remain under personal liability after he has parted with the land, is entitled, even in the absence of an express provision to that effect in the contract of sale, to a covenant from the purchaser to pay the rent and perform and observe the covenants and conditions contained in the instrument creating the rent.[2] The object of such a covenant, however, is not to give the vendor an independent right to sue for a breach of the original covenants, but only to indemnify him against the consequences of the rentowner enforcing such covenants against him. The purchaser is, therefore, entitled to preface his covenant with the words " with the object and intent of affording to the vendor, his executors and administrators, a full and sufficient indemnity, but not further or otherwise," although,

---

[1] *Jones v Kearney,* 1 Dr and War 155.

[2] *Re Poole & Clarke* (1904), 2 Ch 173

even if these words were omitted, the covenant would be restricted to one of indemnity.[1]

Effect of conveyance of the land upon the rentowner's remedies.

It must, however, be remembered that the existence of such a covenant as is now referred to does not give *to the rentowner* any additional remedy against the purchaser,[2] though if there be a continuous chain of indemnifying covenants the original covenantor can, if he be sued by the rentowner, claim indemnity from the last person on the chain, without making intermediate covenantors parties to his proceedings.[3] It is, again, doubtful whether the burden of a covenant to pay a rentcharge runs with the land.[4] But, although a purchaser may not be liable in covenant, every person in whom the whole,[5] or any part of,[6] the land which is subject to the rentcharge is vested is liable in debt to the owner of the rent for arrears of rent accruing during the period in which it is so vested in him. This liability to be sued in debt is not displaced by the fact that the terre tenant does not receive profits out of the land equivalent to the amount of the rentcharge,[7] but the liability

---

[1] *Re Poole & Clarke* ubi sup *Harris v Boots, Cash Chemists* (1904) 2 Ch 376

[2] *Butler v Butler* 5 Ves 534 re *Errington* (1894), 1 Q B 11 *Bonner v Tottenham Building Society* (1899) 1 Q B 161

[3] *Moule v Garrett*, L R 7 Ex 101

[4] *Brewster v Kidgill* 12 Leon 167 *Salk* 198 *Roach v Wadham*, 6 East 289 *Sugd V & P*

p 594 (14th ed) The purchaser will be bound by restrictive covenants of which he has notice Ante p

Thomas v Sylvester L R 8 I B 368 *Searle v Cook*, 43 Ch D 519

[6] *Christie v Barker*, 53 L J Q B 537

[7] *Pertwee v Townshend* (1896) 2 Q B 129, not following *Odlum v Thompson*, 31 L R Ir 394

does not extend to a mere occupier of the land,[1] or to a liquidator of a Company owning the land,[2] or to a lessee of the landowner[3]—at least if they do not receive equivalent profits out of the land.

Sometimes, instead of selling in consideration of a sum in gross, the owner of the land which is subject to the rent prefers to sell in consideration of a new, or second, chief rent, larger in amount than the first rent. In this case all the points indicated in Chapter I. must be attended to, and the vendor will covenant with the purchaser to pay the first, or over-riding, rent, and to indemnify him against the consequences of his omission to do so. The purchaser will nevertheless be liable to be distrained upon[4] or sued for the over-riding rent, and as a protection against this liability he is usually given, in addition to the vendor's covenant of indemnity, a right, in the event of his being compelled to pay the over-riding rent, to retain and re-imburse himself out of the second rent. Inasmuch as, in such a case as we are now considering, the second rent will always be larger than the over-riding rent, this power of retention has always been considered a sufficient protection to the purchaser. It is essential, however, that

Sale in consideration of a second rent

---

[1] *Swift* v *Kelly*, 24 L R Ir 478

[2] *Re Blackburn & District Benefit Building Society*, 43 Ch D 343

[3] *Re Herbage Rents, Greenwich* (1896), 2 Ch 811

[4] The owner of the first rent would appear, however, to have no priority over the owner of the second rent in respect of distress (Lumley on Annuities, 383), but he would have a prior right to possession

this power of retention should be expressly conferred by the deed, for it is submitted that no
such right will be implied.

Risks of purchasing part of a plot subject to an apportioned part of a second rent

Moreover, although a power of retention is
sufficient indemnity to the owner of the whole plot
of land out of which the first rent issues, it sometimes happens that such owner will sell off a portion
of the plot subject only to an apportioned part of
the second rent, or even freed from it. In such a
case the power of retention is obviously an insufficient protection to the purchaser of the portion
of the plot, and the vendor must give him some
of the other indemnities suggested in the next
Chapter, unless, as not infrequently happens, the
purchaser is precluded by special condition of
sale from taking any objection to the existence
of the over-riding rent, and compelled to be satisfied
with existing indemnities.[1] The purchaser under
such circumstances is in a not very enviable position,
and it is suggested that legal advisers when acting
for purchasers of land who are to take subject
either to an apportioned part of a second rent or
altogether indemnified against it, ought, when
settling the contract of sale, to be careful not to
preclude the purchaser from requiring a fresh
indemnity against the over-riding rent. There
would appear to be no hardship in requiring the
vendor to give such fresh indemnity, because he
will be protected by his power of retainer.

---

[1] But see *Manifold* v *Johnston* (1902) 1 Ir R 7.

The vendor may, however, prefer that the pur- chaser shall be liable to pay both the first and second rents. For instance, if the first rent is £10 and the vendor desires to sell for a receivable rent of £20, he can adopt one of two courses—he can either convey in consideration of a new rent of £30, and himself covenant to pay the £10 rent, or he can convey subject to the rent of £10 and in consideration of a second rent of £20. The first course is, however, preferable from the point of view of the vendor. A second rent has not the same market value as a first rent, whereas, if the former course be adopted the net rent of £20 will probably fetch in the market the same price as a first rent of equivalent amount. There is also another objection to the second course, and that is that if the owner of a second rent were to pay the first rent in order to save the land from being re-entered upon, there might be some difficulty as to his remedies against a successor in title of the original purchaser of the land.[1]

Freehold lands subject to a rent charge may be disclaimed by the trustee in bankruptcy of the terre tenant under sect. 55 of the Bankruptcy Act, 1883.[2] It was held in *re Mercer and Moore*,[3] under the old bankruptcy law, that the legal estate in the land upon such disclaimer vested in the

---

[1] It is submitted, however, that he would be entitled to a charge on the land within the principle of such cases as *Thorne* v *Cann* (1895) A C 11.

[2] 46 & 47 Vict c 52

[3] 14 Ch D 287

Crown, but possibly under the Act of 1883 the Court might make a vesting order.[1] In any case the land would, *semble*, remain subject to the rent.

Stamp duty.

Upon a conveyance of land subject to a rent, *ad valorem* duty is payable on the amount of the purchase money if the consideration be a gross amount, or upon twenty times the second rent created if the consideration be a rent. No additional stamp duty is payable by reason of the land being conveyed subject to the original rent.[2]

---

[1] Williams on Bankruptcy, 9th ed , p 297.

[2] *Swayne v. Commissioners of Stamps* (1900), 1 Q. B. 172

CHAPTER III.

CONVEYANCE OF PART OF A PLOT OF LAND SUBJECT TO A RENTCHARGE.

IN the last chapter we dealt with the case of the owner of land subject to a rent conveying the whole of the land subject to the entire rent. Greater difficulties arise when the landowner desires to sell only a part of such land. Thus :—

The various schemes adopted on selling a portion of land subject to a rent

a   *b*   *c*   *d*

The whole plot is subject to a rent of, say, £20 a year, and the landowner having improved the property, desires to sell the plots separately. His scheme may take one of five shapes :—

(1) He may desire to sell all four plots at one and the same time, each subject to one-fourth of the rent—that is, subject to an apportioned rent of £5 per plot ; or,

(2) He may desire to apportion the rent as in the first case, but to sell the plots at different times ; or,

(3) Instead of selling for a gross sum, he may desire to realise his profit by creating a new and improved rent upon each plot. For instance, he may wish to sell each plot subject to a rent of,

Chap III say, £15, and himself pay the over-riding rent of £20, thus obtaining a net receivable rent of £40; or,

(4) He may desire to throw the entire rent of £20 upon, say, plot (*a*) and sell plots (*b*), (*c*), and (*d*) for gross sums free from any liability in respect of the rent; or,

(5) He may desire to throw the entire rent of £20 upon plot (*a*) and sell plots (*b*), (*c*), and (*d*) in consideration of rents of, say, £10 each, but free from any liability in respect of the rent of £20.

Each plot will be subject to the whole rent unless legally apportioned

The problem to be solved in each case is as to the method by which a purchaser of any plot is to be effectually protected against being called upon to pay either the whole of the over-riding rent of £20 or a greater proportion than that to which he takes subject; for, unless the rent is legally apportioned with the consent of the owner thereof, the owner of any part of the land out of which the rent issues can be either distrained upon,[1] or sued,[2] for the whole amount of the rent, whilst if the deed creating the rent contains a power of absolute re-entry he incurs the additional risk of forfeiting his land by reason of default in payment of his proper proportion of the rent by the owner of another plot

The right of contribution

A word may here be said as to the remedies of the owners of the various plots *inter se* apart

[1] Gilbert 152   [2] *Christie v Barker* 53 L J
                              Q B 537

from, or in the absence of, express remedies conferred by their deeds. It is submitted that the owner of any plot paying in excess of his proper share of the over-riding rent has a right of action for contribution against the owners of the other plots.[1] The case of *Johnson* v. *Wyld*[2] is sometimes cited as an authority against the existence of such a right, but the point of that case was that the claim was by the assignee of part of lands included in a lease against a *sub-lessee* of another part, the latter being under no direct liability to the head landlord. But inasmuch as the owners of portions of lands subject to a rentcharge are all liable to be sued by the rentowner,[3] it is submitted that both upon the common law principle, based upon a common liability to be sued, and the equitable principle based upon community of interest in the subject matter to which a burden is attached,[4] a right to contribution by the owner of part of land subject to a rentcharge who has paid the whole rentcharge from the owners of other parts so subject is clear— and in equity he might perhaps assert his claim to contribution even prior to payment.[5] Moreover,

---

[1] *Christie* v *Barker*, 53 L J Q B at p 542 *Booth* v *Smith*, 14 Q B D 318 *Purtwee* v *Townshend* (1896) 2 Q B at p 133 *Gallagher* v *Nasmith* 12 L T Journal 480 Cary 121, 137

[2] 44 Ch D 146 See also *Hunter* v *Hunt* (1845) 1 C B 300)

[3] *Christie* v *Barker* ubi sup

[4] As to the distinction between the legal and the equitable rights to contribution see per Vaughan Williams L J in *Bonner* v *Tottenham Building Society* (1899) 1 Q B at p 174

[5] *Bolmerhausen* v *Gullick* (1893) 2 Ch 514

if the owner of one plot paid the rent in order to prevent the rentowner enforcing his right of forfeiture, the right to contribution might be enforced on the principle of salvage.[1] In addition to his right to claim against the owners of the other plots personally, the payer of the whole rent might perhaps claim a charge against the other plots on the principle that, where a part owner of property pays off a charge upon the whole, the charge will in equity be kept alive for his benefit.[2]

Value of plots is the basis of contribution

Another point is—assuming a right of contribution to exist—upon what basis the amount of contribution is to be determined, whether upon the basis of the respective values of the several plots or upon the basis of acreage ? It would seem that the proper basis is the value of the plots at the date when the over-riding rent is paid.[3] If this be so, the amount of contribution payable by any particular plot might vary from time to time, and thus render a fresh action for contribution necessary every time the over-riding rent is paid.

Legal apportionment

It is obvious, therefore, that it is better for a purchaser to obtain an express indemnity than to rely on any implied indemnity. The only com-

---

[1] *Allison* v *Jenkins* (1904) 1 Ir Rep 341

[2] *Burrell* v *Egremont*, 7 Beav 205 *Morley* v *Morley*, 5 D M & G 610 *Adams* v *Angell* 5 Ch D 634 *Thorne* v *Cann* (1895) A C 11 *Liquidation*

Estates Co v *Willoughby* (1896), 1 Ch 726, (1898) A C 321

[3] *Allison* v *Jenkins* ubi sup. *Hartley* v *Maddocks* (1899), 2 Ch 199 and see *Ley* v *Ley*, L R 6 Eq 174

plete safeguard against liability to pay more than
his proper proportion of the over-riding rent is to
obtain a legal apportionment of it, with the consent,
that is to say, of the owner of the rent and of the
respective owners of the several portions of land
out of which the rent issues. Upon such a legal
apportionment a purchaser could insist in the
absence of agreement to the contrary, though if
the contract stated that he was only to be " indemnified " against the over-riding rent this would
probably be sufficient to preclude him from requiring a legal apportionment.[1] At common law
there were difficulties attending a legal apportionment, consequent upon the rule that a rentcharge
issues out of the whole and every portion of the
land upon which the same is charged, so that if the
rentowner released any part of the land from the
whole, or any part of, the rent, the entire rent was
extinguished.[2] The practical inconveniences re-
sulting from this rule have now been, to some
extent, removed by sect. 10 of the Law of Property
Amendment Act, 1859,[3] which provides that the
release from a rentcharge of part of the hereditaments charged therewith shall not extinguish the
whole rentcharge, but shall operate only to bar
the right to recover any part of the rentcharge
out of the hereditaments released, without prejudice nevertheless to the rights of all persons

[1] Copinger 615 *re Doherty*, 15
L R Ir 247

[2] Gilbert 154 Co Litt 148.
see further Chapter vi post
[3] 22 & 23 Vict c 35

interested in the hereditaments remaining un-released and not concurring in, or confirming, the release.[1] If, therefore, the rentowner is able and willing to concur, a legal apportionment can be obtained by his releasing each plot from the portion of the rent of £20 to which it is to be no longer subject.

The usual indemnities where a legal apportionment cannot be obtained

A legal apportionment, however, of a rentcharge is comparatively rarely obtainable in practice, and, in default, other means must be devised for indemnifying the purchasers of the several lots. The most usual indemnities are : (1) Mutual covenants by the owners of the various lots to pay their proper proportion of the over-riding rent and to indemnify each other against the consequences of default in payment, and, sometimes, all sums of money which may become due under these covenants are charged upon the plot of the defaulter ; (2) powers of distress over land in respect of which default has been made ; (3) powers of entry for perception of the rents and profits of the same land; (4) creation of new rents by way of indemnity ; (5) assignment of existing rents, by way of indemnity, and (6) grant of a power to collect existing rents, by way of indemnity.[2]

The contract ought always to state what form

---

[1] As to this section see *Booth v Smith*, 14 Q B D 318 *Price v John* (1905), 1 Ch 714, and Chapter vi post

[2] This form of indemnity appears to have increased in popularity in recent years but the writer has grave doubts as to its efficacy See post p 56

the indemnity is to assume. Where the contract
provided that each lot should be sold " with right
of indemnity against the other lots " save as to its
apportioned rent, the purchasers were held to be
entitled to powers of distress and entry to secure
their indemnity.[1]

Whatever express rights of indemnity are given Indemni
they ought always to be expressly assigned with ties ought
to be
the plot to which they are attached, for it is not assigned.
certain that the benefit of them will run with the
land.[2]

A few remarks may here be made upon the Cross
powers of
question of the validity of cross powers of entry and entry and
distress
distress. Mr. Lewis was of opinion that these and the
rule
powers do not fall within the rule against perpetui- against
perpetui-
ties, and that there is no distinction between such ties
powers given by way of indemnity and similar
powers given to a rentowner for securing his rent.[3]
Mr. Gray also considers that they may possibly
be supported upon the ground that they are given
by way of remedy only,[4] and the cases of *Gilbertson*
v. *Richards*,[5] and *Morgan* v. *Davey*[6] afford some
support to this view. Doubt has, however, been
cast upon the correctness of these decisions by the
cases of *London and South-western Railway* v.

---

[1] *Re Doherty* 15 L R Ir 247
and see *Manifold* v *Johnston*
(1902) 1 Ir R 7
[2] *Ante* p 32
[3] *Lewis on Perpetuities* 619
Cop 64 68.

[4] *Gray on Perpetuities* sects
273a, 329
[5] 4 H & N. 277 5 H & N.
453
[6] 1 Cab. & E 114

Gomm[1] and *Dunn v. Flood*,[2] and many prac-
titioners deem it safer to limit the operation of
these powers to the perpetuity period, or such
further period as may not be contrary to the law
against perpetuities.[3] It is, nevertheless, submitted that these powers do not infringe the rule
in question, provided they are only given as a
remedy against non-payment of the rent, and not
against breach of the covenants.   One of the reasons
for considering that similar powers given to a rentowner for the security of the rent need not be
confined to the perpetuity period was that such
remedies form part of the estate in the rent, and
are a present interest in the land.[4] The same
reasoning seems to apply to cross powers of entry
and distress, as the apportioned rents are charges
on the separate lots, and confer a present interest
in the land '

**Powers of
distress
and the
Bills of
Sale Acts**

It is not infrequently asserted that cross powers
of distress are invalid because the instrument conferring them does not comply with the provisions
of the Bills of Sale Acts, 1878[6] and 1882,[7] and
consequently some conveyancers advise their
omission.   It is submitted that such a suggestion
is without foundation   In construing the Bills of
Sale Acts it is always proper to bear in mind what

[1] 20 Ch D 562
[2] 25 Ch D 629
  See *Edwards v Edwards*
(1909) A C 275
[4] Ante p 17

Farrer Conditions of Sale
183 (2nd Ed)
[6] 41 & 42 Vict c 31
[7] 45 & 46 Vict c 43

the mischief was which the Acts were intended to remedy. The object of the Acts was to prevent secret pledges for money lent,[1] and there are documents which the wording of the Acts might be wide enough to include, but which have been held to fall outside the scope of the Acts, having regard to their manifest objects.[2] It is apprehended that a power of distress by way of indemnity against an over-riding rent ought never to be given except over land which is already subject to liability to pay that rent, and if several plots of land are subject to one rent there is, as we have seen,[3] nothing to prevent the rentowner from distraining upon any one of the plots for the whole rent, to the exclusion of the other plots. An arrangement therefore whereby the owners of the various plots agree that as between themselves the whole rent shall be paid out of one plot in exoneration of the other plots, and that the owners of the latter plots, if compelled to pay the rent, shall have such a right of distress over the former plot as the rentowner could undoubtedly have exercised over the same plot if he had so chosen, can hardly be said to fall within the mischief of the Bills of Sale Acts.

But, it is submitted, that not only are these powers of distress not within the spirit of the Bills of Sale Acts, but they are not within the letter. Sects. 4 and 6 of the Act of 1878 are the material

---

[1] Per Lindley L. J. in *Round-wood Colliery Co* (1897) 1 Ch at p 390

[2] *Re Standard Manufacturing Co* (1891) 1 Ch 645

[3] *Ante* p 40

sections.　　By sect. 4 a " bill of sale " is defined to include " licences to take possession of personal chattels *as security for any debt*, and also any agreement, whether intended or not to be followed by the execution of any other instrument, by which a right in equity to any personal chattels or to any charge or security thereon shall be conferred." A power of distress does not confer any right in equity to any personal chattels or any charge or security thereon—the right, if any, is in law—nor is there any debt—or, at least, any present debt—where the power is given by way of indemnity against the non-fulfilment by another of his obligations.[1] The power is not given to secure the rent, which belongs to the rentowner, who is no party to the transaction. but to secure the performance of his agreement by the owner of the plot upon which the rent is charged in exoneration of the other plots. Moreover, inasmuch as sect 6 of the same Act contains express provisions as to powers of distress, and sect. 4 does not, the reasonable inference seems to be that sect. 4 was not intended to apply to such powers at all

Sect. 6 provides that " every attornment instrument or agreement, not being a mining lease, whereby a power of distress is given or agreed to be given by any person to any other person by way of security for any present, future, or contingent debt or advance, and whereby any rent is reserved

---

[1] See *ex parte* Newitt, 16 Ch D 522

or made payable as a mode of providing for the payment of interest on such debt or advance or otherwise for the purpose of such security only, shall be deemed a Bill of Sale." This section does expressly refer to powers of distress to secure future or contingent debts, but it is submitted that a right of indemnity is not, strictly speaking, a debt at all, but only gives rise to a possible claim for unliquidated damages. Moreover, a power of distress for securing a debt is not, by the terms of the section, to be a Bill of Sale unless a " rent is reserved or made payable as a mode of providing for the payment of interest on such debt or advance," and the instruments we are now considering never do reserve any such rent. The cases of *Green* v *Marsh*[1] and *Pulbrook* v. *Ashby*[2] are the cases usually cited as authorities against the validity of these powers of distress, but both cases are clearly distinguishable. In the former case an attornment clause in a mortgage deed which reserved a rent to the mortgagee slightly in excess of the interest on the mortgage debt was held void under the Bills of Sale Acts, but the amount of both principal and interest was clearly fixed and the deed did reserve a rent. *Pulbrook* v. *Ashby* is even less in point, for the power of distress there held to be invalid was given for the recovery of the price of goods sold. On the other hand, in the case of *re Roundwood Colliery*

---

[1] (1892) 2 Q B 330.   [2] 56 L J Q B 376

D

Company[1] it was held that a power contained in a mining lease to distrain for rent upon land adjoining the demised premises did not fall within the provisions of the Bills of Sale Acts. Although this case may not be precisely in point, its reasoning goes some way towards establishing the validity of powers of distress given by way of indemnity against an over-riding rent.[2]

But it is at least clear that, even if such powers are invalid, their invalidity does not affect the other provisions of the deeds containing them,[3] and it is therefore thought that until the question of their validity or invalidity has been decided by the Courts, it is certainly proper to insert them for what they are worth.

Some conveyancers consider that the most effective protection that can be provided against an over-riding rent is to create a new rent by way of indemnity out of the indemnifying plot[4] One objection to this form of indemnity is that the amount of the indemnifying rent must be fixed, whereas it is obviously impossible to know beforehand what precisely will be the amount necessary to indemnify the person who has been compelled to pay the over-riding rent. If the indemnifying

---

[1] (1897) 1 Ch 373
[2] See 5 Jarm & Byth 635 for an argument in favour of the validity of cross powers of distress—an argument which so far as the writer is aware, has never been attempted to be answered

[3] *Ex parte Birm* 20 Q B D 310 315 *Ex parte Mason* (1895) 1 Q B 333
[4] *Casamajor* v *Strode* 2 Swanst 347

rent be fixed at too low a figure, the owner of the indemnified lot may suffer; if it be fixed at too high a figure, the owner of the indemnifying lot may suffer. Moreover, if the plots to be indemnified are at all numerous it will be necessary to vest the rent in a trustee on behalf of all the owners of indemnified plots, whereas powers of distress and entry can be readily given to any number of persons.

In order to avoid any question of perpetuity, an indemnifying rent is generally limited so as to commence immediately upon the execution of the instrument creating it, and not so as to arise when default has been made by the owner of the indemnifying lot [1] It may be provided that payment of the rent shall not be compelled except for the purpose of re-couping losses that may arise from non-payment of the over-riding rent, or a provision may be inserted—as advised by Mr. Lewis[2]—that the payment of the over-riding rent shall be taken and deemed to be a payment of the indemnifying rent, and entitle the grantor to a receipt It is submitted that such an indemnifying rent will not be statute-barred in twelve years, although it may never, in fact, have been paid [3]

With these preliminary remarks, we are in a position to consider the various methods of effecting the objects referred to on p. 39

---

[1] Lewis on Perpetuities. p 612 Gilb 60

[2] p 613

[3] See Chapter vi post

1. The usual course in this case is to have one conveyance to all four purchasers, each purchaser covenanting with the other purchasers and the vendor to pay his apportioned part of the over-riding rent, and to indemnify the owners of the other lots and the vendor, and granting to the other purchasers powers of distress and entry in the event of his failing to pay his proper share.[1] The conveyance will be executed in quadruplicate, and provision must be made in the contract as to the custody of the other title deeds. If any lot fails to find a purchaser, the vendor usually enters into similar covenants and gives similar powers over the unsold lot. If preferred, there may be four distinct conveyances, and the mutual covenants and powers of entry and distress inserted in a separate deed

Another scheme is for each purchaser to grant a rentcharge of, say, double the amount of his apportioned rent, by way of indemnity, but in such a case as the present, where there are more than two lots, the indemnifying rents had better be granted to a trustee on behalf of the several purchasers

2 This scheme may be carried out in a some-what similar manner to the first Plot (*a*) will be conveyed to the purchaser subject to its appor-tioned rent of £5 The purchaser will covenant to pay this rent and give to the vendor a power of entry and distress in case of default : the vendor

covenanting with the purchaser to pay the residue of the rent and giving a power of entry and distress over lots (b), (c), and (d). Upon the sale of lots (b) and (c), the same course is followed, the vendor covenanting to indemnify against £15 and giving powers over lots (c) and (d) in the one case, and over lot (d) alone in the other case. Upon the sale of the last lot the vendor cannot give any further powers, but he assigns to the purchaser of this lot the benefit of the powers given by the purchasers of the other three lots. Although there are other schemes for securing the various purchasers, this is the scheme most usually adopted, and the rights of the various parties in the event of their being called upon to pay more than their proper proportion may be gathered from the table printed on the following page.[1]

If at the date of his first sale the vendor has finally determined his scheme of apportionment, the apportionment might be secured by granting to a trustee new and distinct rents out of the various plots by way of indemnity.

3. The difficulty as to this scheme lies in the fact that the various purchasers are to be liable to pay no part of the over-riding rent, and must be completely indemnified against it. The vendor will covenant with each purchaser to pay the over-

[1] Sometimes the vendor on the sale of plot (b) and the subsequent plots assigns the benefit of powers given over plots previously sold, so far as may be necessary to indemnify each plot but upon the whole, the plan suggested in the text is to be preferred

Table showing remedy of an owner of a plot subject to an apportioned rent being compelled to pay the whole rent [1]

Person liable to pay whole rent	Owners of —				REMEDIES
	Lot a	Lot b	Lot c	Lot d	
(1) Vendor	A	Vendor	Vendor	Vendor	A's covenant and power of distress over lot (a)
Vendor	A	B	Vendor	Vendor	A's and B's covenant and powers of distress over Lots (a) and (b)
Vendor	A	B	C	Vendor	A's, B's and C's covenant and powers of distress over Lots (a), (b) and (c)
Vendor	A	B	C	D	A's, B's, C's and D's covenant
(2) A	A	Vendor	Vendor	Vendor	Vendor's covenant and power of distress for £15 over lots (b), (c) and (d)
(3) A	A	B	Vendor	Vendor	A has vendor's covenant and power of distress over lots (b), (c) and (d). B, if distrained on, his vendor's covenant and power of distress over lots (c) and (d). Vendor has B's covenant and a power of distress over lot (b)
(4) A	A	B	C	Vendor	A has the same remedies as in (3) and (5). B has the same remedies as in (5). C has vendor's covenant and power of distress over (d). Vendor has B's and C's covenant and power of distress over (b) and (c)
(5) A	A	B	C	D	A, B and C have the same remedies as in (4). D has vendor's covenant and the powers of distress over lots (b) and (c) granted to vendor by B and C respectively. Vendor has covenants of B, C and D
(6) B	A	B	C	Vendor	B has vendor's covenant and power of distress over lots (c) and (d) for the residue (£15) of the rent. The vendor has A's covenant and power of distress over lot (a) for £5
(7) B	A	B	C	Vendor	B has same remedies as in (6). C has vendor's covenant and a power of distress over lot (d). Vendor has A's and C's covenant and power of distress over lots (a) and (c)
(8) B	A	B	C	D	A, B and C have the same remedies as in (7). D has vendor's covenant and vendor's power of distress over lots (a) and (c). Vendor has covenants of A, C and D
(9) C	A	B	C	Vendor	C has vendor's covenant and a power of distress over lot (d) for the residue (£15). Vendor has A's and B's covenant and power of distress over their lots
(10) C	A	B	C	D	C has same remedies as in (9). D has vendor's covenant and power of distress over lots (a) and (b). Vendor has A's, B's and D's covenant
(11) D	A	B	C	D	D has vendor's covenant and power of distress over lots (a), (b) and (c). Vendor has A's, B's and C's covenants

(1) He may, perhaps have in addition the implied remedies referred to on p. 41 ante.

riding rent and empower him, if called upon to pay it, to retain the rent of £15 payable by him to the vendor. This power of retention is an effectual indemnity so far as it goes,[1] but inasmuch as the new rent is less than the over-riding rent the purchaser will require a further indemnity for his protection, and this is usually provided by giving him powers of distress and entry over the remaining portion of the land retained by the vendor. Thus, upon selling plot (*a*) the vendor gives powers of distress and entry over plots (*b*), (*c*), and (*d*). When the vendor comes to sell plot (*b*) he can, of course, confer no rights over plot (*a*), but he can give powers of distress and entry over plots (*c*) and (*d*), and similarly on the sale of plot (*c*) he can give like powers over plot (*d*). Greater difficulty arises with regard to the last plot, upon which the whole rent of £20 is now charged, although the vendor is entitled to receive out of the other plots rents amounting to £45 in all. Inasmuch as £20 may be too high a rent for plot (*d*), and the rents of £15 secured upon plots (*a*) (*b*) and (*c*) are second rents subject to powers of retention—and consequently not readily saleable separately—the usual course is for the vendor to sell plot (*d*) subject to the whole over-riding rent, but to include in the sale the three second rents of £15, the purchaser thus acquiring the last plot together with a net receivable

---

[1] Express power of retention must, it is thought, be given. Such a power would not be implied.

rent of £25. The alternative to this course is to assign one or more of the second rents to a trustee upon trust to indemnify the purchaser. Occasionally, instead of assigning the second rents to a trustee a power of attorney is given to the purchaser to collect the second rents himself, if called upon to pay the over-riding rent: but this latter form of indemnity is not to be recommended, for although under sect. 8 of the Conveyancing Act, 1882,[1] such a power can be made irrevocable, it is doubtful whether the benefit of such a power can pass with the indemnified land, and still more doubtful whether an assignee of the rents to be collected would be bound by a power of collection, whether he had, or had not, notice of the existence of such power.

Entire rent thrown on one plot and other plots sold for gross sums

4. This arrangement is carried out by a conveyance of plot (*a*) subject to and charged with the entire rent, in exoneration of the remaining plots. The purchaser of this plot covenants to pay the rent, charges it upon his plot in exoneration of the others, and gives powers of distress and entry over his plot to the purchasers of the other plots [2] If the vendor himself retains plot (*a*) he will covenant to pay the rent and give, directly, powers of distress and entry to the purchasers of the other plots; but if he sells plot (*a*) first, then

---

[1] 45 & 46 Vict c 39
[2] A simple covenant to pay the whole rent may be ineffec-
tual, if the burden of this covenant does not run with the land, see ante p 34

on the sales of the other plots he will assign to the various purchasers the benefit of the powers over plot (*a*) so far as may be necessary to indemnify their respective plots.

Another method of carrying out this arrangement is for the purchaser of plot (*a*) to grant a second rent out of his plot to a trustee for the purpose of indemnifying the purchasers of the other plots.[1]

5. This arrangement is merely a variation of the last. The purchaser of plot (*a*) gives similar covenants and powers. No powers of retention in respect of their respective rents of £10 will be given to the purchasers of plots (*b*), (*c*), and (*d*), but they will have to rely on their rights against the owner of plot (*a*) in the event of their being compelled to pay the over-riding rent. In an arrangement of this character these rents of £10 are known as "indemnified second chiefs," and although, strictly speaking, they are only second rents, they are regarded in the market as something better—provided the income of plot (*a*) is considerably greater than the over-riding rent—and usually sell for as good a price as first rents.

If the vendors are trustees or mortgagees, it is conceived that they are at liberty to adopt either the first or second scheme referred to on p. 39, but that they cannot adopt either the third or fifth scheme, unless they have been given express

[1] *Casamajor v Strode 2 Swanst 347*

powers to sell in consideration of a rentcharge.[1]
It is not clear whether trustees or mortgagees
could adopt the fourth scheme, but in practice
it is frequently done without objection. Trustees,
by virtue of sect. 13 of the Trustee Act, 1893,[2]
and mortgagees, by virtue of sect. 19 of the Con
veyancing Act, 1881,[3] are empowered to sell
either altogether or in lots, all or any part of the
property subject to the trust or mortgage, by
public auction or private contract, and subject to
such conditions respecting title or evidence of title
or other matters as they may think fit. Having
therefore, a power to sell in lots, it is submitted that
it follows that trustees and mortgagees are im
pliedly authorised to apportion the rent amongst
the plots as they may consider advisable, and to
give all such power and remedie to the purchaser
of any lot to protect him against his liability to
pay more than his proper proportion of the rent.
It however submitted that a prudent mortga
and mortgagee will avoid subjecting him to
restraint to payment of the part apportioned to
expected title that the part of the apportioned
to and the prop part the may be owner
the purchaser and the part or
to be that if the part the prop
part the the prop part

unless he is precluded by the conditions of sale, but the purchaser's only remedy would be rescission. He, probably, could not compel trustees to give unqualified covenants.[1]

A tenant for life, selling under the Settled Land Acts a portion of land which is subject to a rent charge, can exonerate the part sold by obtaining the consent of the owner of the rentcharge to charging the whole of it upon the unsold portion under sect. 5 of the Settled Land Act, 1882, but it is considered doubtful whether he could do so without the concurrence of the rentowner.

CHAPTER IV.

CONVEYANCES OF EXISTING RENTS.

Description of rentcharge in particulars of sale.

WHERE a rentcharge is to be sold, care should be taken to accurately describe it in the particulars of sale. The expressions "ground rent," "freehold ground rent," "leasehold ground rent," are applicable only to rents incident to a reversion, a freehold ground rent having a freehold reversion, and a leasehold ground rent having a leasehold reversion. A chief rent may properly be described as "All that perpetual yearly rentcharge of £ issuing out of all that plot of land situate &c." A misdescription of the land upon which the rent was charged might entitle the purchaser to rescind the contract.

It would of course be a gross misdescription to sell a ground rent without disclosing, at the time, to the purchaser that it was a ground rent. A ground rent is liable to be avoided, subject to rights of

and are consequently often considered in the market
as being equal in security to first rents ; but even
on the sale of such indemnified rents it is proper to
indicate that the lands out of which they issue
are subject to an over riding rent.

By reason of the rights of retainer to which
second rents are subject, a second rent is generally
only saleable subject to the first rent, the purchaser
in such a case covenanting with the vendor to pay
the first rent and to indemnify him against the
consequences of his failure to do so. But if a second
rent is for any reason sold free from the first rent
the purchaser must be indemnified against the
event of the payee of the second rent exercising
his power of retainer. The most usual form of
indemnity is for the vendor to assign other rent
to which he is entitled, to a trustee to hold upon
trust to indemnify the purchaser but sometimes
the purchaser is content with a power of attorney
to collect such other rents if and when it is
for the purpose of indemnifying him, the latter form of indemnity is preferred.

A vendor

tenant before he could be distrained upon,¹ and though attornment is no longer necessary the fiction is still maintained. It is, however, undesirable to split up a rent in this manner, because, although the right to distrain is not affected, a power of entry is indivisible, and a severance thereof by act of the parties, as distinct from an act of law, will have the effect of destroying the power.²

If, however, the rent be conveyed to two as tenants in common, or descend to two as co-parceners the powers of entry are not extinguished, but probably are not exerciseable by one tenant in common, or one co-parcener, without the other of them. To avoid the difficulty that might otherwise arise, if one tenant in common should do so to exercise the power of entry without the other it will be advisable when any entire rent is to be conveyed to two tenant the intention to convey a several apt in and to create the power to the apt of the tenant in common in other of them.

tenant in common after he has received notice from the other tenant not to do so.[1]

An objection to title not infrequently arising upon the sale of an existing rent is that the lands and houses upon which the rent is secured are subject to an exception of mines and minerals with power for the owner of the mines to let down the surface. Even if in the deed excepting the mines there are provisions for compensating the surface owner in the event of damage being occasioned, it will seldom happen that the compensation will be payable to the rentowner. Under such circumstances, therefore, a vendor should insert a special clause in his contract of sale precluding the purchaser from raising any objection on this ground, and if it can be ascertained that the minerals are being worked at a very low level the fact might be pointed out as being a matter tending to improve the purchase price.

A conveyance of an existing rent may be effected so as to operate either at common law or under the Statute of Uses. If at common law it is effectual to pass the legal estate in the rent, the grantor being a person entitled thereto in possession, either for his own benefit or as trustee for another, and the grant being duly completed by attornment of the person liable to the payment of the rent.

Chap. IV. rent.[1] The rules applicable to conveyances of corporeal hereditaments must be observed in conveying freehold rents, and, in particular, a future freehold estate or interest in an existing rent cannot be granted by deed, unless such estate or interest be either supported by a particular estate of freehold or limited by way of springing or shifting use.[2]

If the rent be in arrear at the date of the conveyance, the arrears must be expressly assigned, for, if they are not, neither the grantee[3] nor the grantor[4] can distrain for them; but if the land owner has paid the rent in advance, this is not a discharge of the rent, and the purchaser of the rent can require payment as it falls due.

The question whether the benefit of the land owner's covenants will run with the rent is one of some difficulty, the authorities on the point being indecisive and conflicting. We have already dealt with the question whether the *burden* of covenant runs with the land, and the conclusion to which we arrived was that until the burden of a positive covenant could run with the land. It is admitted that the question whether the *benefit* of the covenants entered into with an original covenantee passes with the rent does not turn upon any question of whether the covenants are positive or negative. Whether the benefit of covenants runs with *land* turns upon whether or not the covenants relate, touch, or concern the land claiming the benefit thereof. It may be doubtful whether building and other similar covenants do relate, touch, or concern the rent,—but it is submitted that no such doubt can exist as to the covenant to pay the rent, and that if the benefit of such a covenant does not run with the rent it must be because no covenant can run with a rent, as distinguished from *land*. But that the benefit of a covenant can run with an incorporeal hereditament is decided in *Holly v. Wells,* a case of tithe, and in *Brewster v. Kidgill* it was assumed that the benefit of a covenant to pay a rentcharge ran with the rent. However, in the case of *Milnes v. Branch*, Lord Ellenborough did draw a distinction between land and rent, and although in that case the plaintiff ... ...

Chap. IV.

with a rent.[1] In the above state of the authorities it will, therefore, always be advisable, in conveying a rent, to expressly assign the benefit of the covenants, to which there can be no objection, unless such benefit has been expressly confined to the original covenantee.[2] It is also usual to assign the benefit of all powers and remedies for the recovery of the rent, although it has been held that if such powers are given to the original grantee, his heirs and assigns, they will pass with the rent.[3]

Mortgage of a rent.

A mortgage of a first rent presents no peculiar features, but in the case of a mortgage of a second rent it is usual for the mortgagor to covenant to pay the first rent during the continuance of the security and until sale or foreclosure.[4]

[1] [illegible] 4 M. & W. 130 [illegible] Q.B.D. 103 [illegible]

[illegible] dence of contrary intention to be entered into with the covenantee his heirs and assigns. Conveyancing and Law of Property Act, 1881 [illegible]

[illegible]

CHAPTER V.

SALE OF RENTS TO BE CREATED.

THE rules of equity forbid the creation of perpetual
mortgages, but what is the practical equivalent
of a perpetual mortgage can be created by the
device of granting a rentcharge in consideration
of a gross sum. Moreover, a perpetual rentcharge
has various advantages over a mortgage as an
investment, particularly for trustees, whom recent
decisions have shown are exposed to considerable
personal risks in lending trust moneys upon mortgage security. Landowners, therefore, not infrequently create rentcharges upon other occasions
than the sale of their lands.

Trustees, however, cannot invest trust moneys
upon the *purchase* of chief rents unless expressly
authorised so to do by their trust instrument. A
power to invest on real securities, refers primarily
to mortgages of real property, including of course,
mortgages of chief rents; and although sometimes
the word securities will be construed in a
proper case as including investment of any
character, it cannot be assumed that it will not

Chap V. receive this construction in sect. 4 of the Trustee Act, 1893.[1] A power, however, to invest "upon" chief rents would authorise the purchase of chief rents.[2]

Remedies. As regards the creation of rents otherwise than upon the sale of land and the remedies of the rent-owners for recovery of their rents, the same general principles apply as in the case of a sale of land in consideration of a rent,[3] but it must not be supposed that because trustees, mortgagees, or others requiring special authority to create rents are authorised to sell in consideration of a rent, that they are thereby authorised to grant a rent otherwise than upon sale of the land.

Grant of rent by mortgagor or mortgagee alone. A mortgagor has not such an estate as to enable him to grant a legal rentcharge;[4] but although the rent so created would not bind the mortgagee, it would doubtless bind the mortgagor by way of estoppel. If, on the other hand, a mortgagee granted a rent without the concurrence of the mortgagor, the latter might, on redeeming, avoid the rent.

Creation of the rent. The rent in the circumstances we are now considering may be created either by direct grant or

_____

[footnotes illegible]

through the medium of the Statute of Uses[1]—
that is to say, the grantor may either grant to the
grantee and his heirs a perpetual yearly rentcharge
of £r to be issuing and payable out of the plot of
land, to hold unto and to the use of the grantee, his
heirs and assigns, or he may convey the land to X
and his heirs, to the use that the grantee and his
heirs may receive a perpetual yearly rentcharge of
£r, and subject thereto to the use of the grantor in
fee simple. It is essential in the latter case to insert
a grantee to uses. A mistake that is sometimes
made is for the grantor to grant to the *grantee* and
his heirs to the use that the grantee and his heirs
may receive a rent of £r, &c. This is an ineffective
grant of a rent, not only because the Statute of
Uses only applies where one person is seised to
the use of *another*, but because a man cannot own
a rent issuing out of his own land, and the grantee's
use would merge in his estate.

The method of direct grant is probably more
often employed than a grant operating under the
Statute of Uses, but where the land is in mortgage
it is, perhaps, preferable for the mortgagor and
mortgagee to concur in granting to a grantee to
uses, and where the rent is to be created by tenants
in common it is imperative to make the grant in

---

[1] A rent may of course be created by will but a rent or rentcharge is really grantable to be perpetual, not though it ... fall within the operation of the ... create a rent in fee by will with proper word of limitation as necessary. Noble v Meade ... In Re ... Blyth v Hartwell ... Ch. Div. ...

this way. The reason for this is, that if two tenants in common grant a rent of £x, the grantee will be entitled to two rents of £x, for every man's grant will be construed most strongly against himself, and they are several grants in law.[1]

Joint tenants
granting
rent

Joint tenants, however, have only one joint interest, and therefore if all the joint tenants concur in granting a rent only one rent is created : but if one of two joint tenants grant a rent out of his interest and his co-tenant survives, the rent will only continue during the life of the grantor, and the survivor will hold free from the rent, for he claims by title paramount.[2] To avoid this difficulty the rent should be created by a deed operating under the Statute of Uses, so as to sever the joint tenancy. Moreover, if A and B are joint tenants, and A grants a rent and subsequently releases to B, B will hold subject to the rent, for he does not take by title paramount.[3]

Co par-
ceners
granting
rent

Again, if one of two co-parceners, prior to partition, grants a rent, and then dies intestate and without issue, so that her share descends to the other co-parcener, the latter will hold the land charged with the rent.[4]

And where one co-parcener grants a rent to two

<hr>

[1] Co Litt 197a Windham's *Case* 5 Rep 8 It is said that no language expressive of intention to grant only one rent would be effectual to that end Preston Abst ii p 77 Distinguish this case from the case of a vendor to tenants in common reserving to himself a rent, ante p 7

[2] Co Litt 184b

[3] Ib 185a

[4] Ib 184b

other co-parceners for equality of partition, the grantees are not joint tenants of the rent, but their holding will be in the nature of co-parcenary.[1]

If the land out of which the rent is to be granted is already subject to a first rent, the only security that the grantor can give the grantee against the first rent will be the grantor's personal covenant to pay it. It is, therefore, preferable in such a case for the grantor, unless the security is ample, to grant a second rent equal to the combined first and second rents, and for the grantee to take subject to, and covenant to pay, the first rent. No greater burden is thus imposed upon the grantor, for he can be completely indemnified against being compelled to pay the first rent by a power of retention over the second rent.

A rent cannot be granted out of an incorporeal hereditament, because such a hereditament could not be distrained upon,[2] but such a grant might be held good by way of contract[3]

A lessee cannot, on assigning a lease for the residue of the term, reserve a rent to himself,[4] but there appears to be no objection to a lessee granting a rentcharge out of his leasehold interest,[5] although such a rent could not be perpetual, and would be merely a chattel interest[6] The usual method

---

[1] *Ib* 169b
[2] Co Litt 47a
[3] *Ib*
[4] *Smith* v *Mapleback* 1 T R 441 *Pascoe* v *Pascoe* 3 Bing N C 898 *Preece* v *Corrie* 5 Bing 24 *Lewis* v *Baker* (1905) 1 Ch 46
Co Litt 47b *re Fraser* (1904) 1 Ch 111 72b But see — v *Cooper* 2 Wils 375
[6] 1 Prest Abstr 358

adopted by a lessee who desires to create a rent out of his leasehold interest is to sub-lease to a nominee reserving the rent, and then assign the reversion, with the benefit of the rent, to the purchaser, but in such a case the purchaser frequently only obtains the covenants of a man of straw, and other circumstances often arise rendering a direct grant of a rentcharge preferable. Such a rentcharge is a "chattel real," and will pass under a gift by will of "real estates and chattels real"[1] It also falls under the provisions of the Real Estates Charges Act, 1877,[2] so that it will, in the absence of intention to the contrary, pass to a deceased's legatee or next of kin charged with a primary liability to pay any mortgage or lien that may be subsisting thereon[3]

But where a rent is to be secured upon a leasehold interest there are one or two points to be observed. In the first place, the Statute of Uses does not apply to leaseholds, and therefore the rent must be created by direct grant or reservation. Secondly, it is advisable to insert express powers of distress and entry for the security of the rent, for it is not certain that sect. 44 of the Conveyancing Act, 1881, would be held to apply to a rentcharge issuing out of leaseholds. The section is expressed to apply to rentcharges issuing out of "land," and by sect. 2 of the same Act land is defined as including

---

[1] *re Fraser* ubi supra   [3] *re Fraser* supra
[2] 40 and 41 Vict. c. 34

"land of any tenure," but there is some doubt whether such an expression covers a leasehold interest.[1] Thirdly, it is advisable, if the rentowner is given a power of re-entry for breach of the covenants, to provide that, prior to his doing so, he shall give notice to the grantor and any mortgagee of his of whom he may have written notice, because sect 14 of the Conveyancing Act, 1881, does not appear to be applicable, and the absence of such provision might prejudice the grantor of the rent if he should at any time desire to mortgage his interest

The stamp upon the grant of a rentcharge will be *ad valorem* on the amount of the purchase money, and if the rentcharge is for life only, the deed creating it should be registered under the Judgment Registration Act, 1855[2]

It may here be noted that a rentcharge is subject to dower,[3] and curtesy.[4] If the rent is limited in fee simple, it will descend upon the heir-at-law of the owner if he dies intestate,[5] but if the rent be charged upon lands governed by the custom of gavelkind or borough English, the descent of the

---

[1] Hood and Challis (7th ed.) p 11 Compare the definition of "settled land" in sect 2 sub-sect (3) of the Settled Land Act 1882 (45 & 46 Vict c 38) But see *re Kershaw* '87 Ch D 674

[2] 18 & 19 Vict c 15 ss 12 14
[3] Co Litt 32a
[4] Co Litt 29
If he has no heirs see Intestates Estates Act 1884 (47 & 48 Vict c 71) s 4 and post p 75

rent will be governed by such customs.[1]   The descent of a rent limited *pur autre vie* is governed by the same rules as apply to land limited for a similar estate.[2]

Appor-
tionment
of rent
under
Appor-
tionment
Act, 1870. Under sect. 1 of the Apportionment Act, 1870,[3] a rentcharge is, like interest on money lent, to be considered as accruing from day to day, and apportionable accordingly : but an apportioned part of a rent is not payable until the entire rent of which such apportioned part forms part becomes due and payable,[4] and then the entire rent is to be paid to the person who is at the date of payment entitled to the rent, from whom the persons entitled to the apportioned part may recover such apportioned part by action at law or suit in equity.[5]

[1] *Randall* v *Brittle* 2 Lev. 87 *Stokes* v *Verner* 1 Mod. 112 *Edwin* v *Thomas* 1 Vern. 489, *Smith* v *Lane* 1 And. 191

[2] *Northen* v *Carnegie* 28 L J Ch. 930 *Chadfield* v *Berchtoldt*, L R 7 Ch 192 Wills Act (1 Vict c 26) ss 3, 6

[3] 33 & 34 Vict c 35

[4] Sect 3

[5] Sect 4

CHAPTER VI.

EXTINGUISHMENT OF RENTCHARGES.

THE extinguishment of a rent may be either volun- *Voluntary or in voluntary.* tary or involuntary, by act of law or act of the parties.

A rent will be determined by the termination *By termination of estate.* of the estate of either grantor or grantee of the rent, but the grantor of a rent may not defeat his grant by determining his estate by his own act, *e.g.*, by disentailing or surrendering;[1] and sometimes a rent may be fed by an estoppel, *e q*, if a tenant for life grants a rent in fee and subsequently acquires the remainder.[2]

Prior to the Intestates' Estates Act, 1884,[3] if *Escheat is now to the Crown* the owner in fee of a rentcharge died intestate and without heirs, the rentcharge became extinguished, and sank into the land upon which it was charged,[4] but the meaning of the somewhat obscurely worded enactment above referred to appears to be that, in the event of such an owner so dying after the passing of that Act, the rentcharge does not cease, but escheats to the Crown.

If the rentcharge and the estate out of which it *By merger*

---

[1] *White v West* Cro Eliz 793 *Cage v Acton* 1 Ld Raym 520 Co Litt 338b

[2] *Holt v Sandbach* Cro Car 103

[3] 47 & 48 Vict c 71 s 4

[4] *Challis R P* 2nd ed pp 37 38

Chap VI issues become united in ownership, the rentcharge will generally merge and be extinguished, but " in order that there may be merger the two estates which are supposed to coalesce must be vested in the same person at the same time, and in the same right."[1] If, therefore, the owner of the land be trustee of the rent or vice versa, there will be no merger : or if the rent be granted by a tenant in possession to a remainderman and the latter assigns the rent before his estate falls into possession, the rent will not be extinguished on the remainder subsequently falling in.[2] Nor does a mortgage of the land to the rentowner extinguish the rent[3]

Land and rent held for different estates Moreover, if the estate in the rent be less than the estate in the land, there can, at most, be only a temporary merger, *e.g.*, if a tenant for life of the rent takes a conveyance of the fee simple of the land out of which the rent issues, the rent will only be suspended during the lifetime of the grantee.[4] On the other hand, if the tenant for life of the land obtains a release of the rent to himself, the rent is extinguished at law,[5] for there is but one rent which issues out of both the life estate and the remainder."[6]

---

[1] Per Lindley L J re Rad cliffe (1892) 1 Ch 227
[2] Gouldwell's Case Pop 131 Dutton v Engram Cro Jac 427
[3] Elliot v Hancock 2 Vern 143

[4] Heliot v Sanders Cro Jac. 700 Co Litt 313 a & b Haverington's Case Owen 7
[5] Co Litt 267b
[6] Burrell v Egremont, 7 Beav 205 Morley v Morley 5 D M & G 610

But although the rent will under the circumstances last mentioned be extinguished at law, it is submitted that it will not be extinguished in equity, in the absence of evidence that such is the intention of the parties, for there is an equitable doctrine that where a limited owner, not being the creator of the charge, pays off a charge upon the inheritance, the charge is usually to be kept alive for his benefit. The doctrine, indeed, goes further, and is to the effect that if any purchaser of property pays off a charge on it without showing an express intention to merge it, it will be held in equity to continue as an existing charge, if to so hold would be beneficial to him[1] And there appears to be no difference between merger of charges and merger of estates.[2] If, therefore, the intention of the parties is to merge the rent it is always as well to express this intention on the face of the conveyance.

How entirely the question of merger depends in equity upon intention is illustrated by the case of *re Betton*.[3] There a wife was entitled to a rent-charge out of her husband's lands. She joined with her husband in executing a mortgage of the lands and in the operative part of the deed she was expressed to convey ' for the purpose of

---

[1] *Adams v. Angell* 5 Ch D 634 *Thorne v. Cann* (1895) A C 11 *Liquidation Estates v. Willoughby* (1896) 1 Ch 726 (1898) A C 321

[2] *Ingle v. Vaughan Jenkins* (1900) 2 Ch 368 *Thellusson v. Liddiard* (1900) 2 Ch 635 *Capital & Counties Bank v. Rhodes* (1903) 1 Ch 631

[3] L R 12 Eq 553

absolutely releasing and for ever extinguishing" the rentcharge. The mortgage was subsequently paid off, and the lands re-conveyed to the husband ; but when a successor in title of the husband contracted to sell part of the lands, the Court refused to force the title upon the purchaser, upon the ground that it was not clear that the rentcharge was extinguished except for the purpose of the mortgage, upon payment off of which the rentcharge might have revived. But where an owner in fee simple or in tail takes a conveyance of the rent to himself the presumption will always be in favour of merger.

Rules as to merger now the same in Courts of law and of equity.

It is now provided by the Judicature Act[1] that, where there is any conflict between the rules of equity and of law, the rules of equity are to prevail, and that there shall not be any merger, by operation of law only, of any estate the beneficial interest in which would not be deemed to be merged or extinguished in equity.[2]

Relying upon these provisions a practice has grown up of inserting in a conveyance of a rentcharge to the owner of the land out of which it issues, or vice versa, an express declaration in the deed of an intention against merger, but it is perhaps still preferable, in a case where merger is not desired, to convey the rent to a trustee for the landowner

---

[1] 36 & 37 Vict. c. 66, sect. 25.   [2] Ib. sub-s. (4)
sub-s. (11)

A release to one of two tenants in common[1] or to the terre tenant and a stranger[2] operates to extinguish one-half of the rent only; but a release may be made of part of a rentcharge, *e.g.*, £5 out of a rent of £10, without extinguishing the rent.[3] A release, however, to one of two joint tenants will no doubt generally operate to extinguish the whole rent, but it has been suggested that the joint tenant might elect to keep it alive.[4]

Inasmuch as a rentcharge issues out of the whole of the land upon which it is charged, and, as it was said, is against common right, if the rentowner released any part of the land from the rent, the rule was that the whole rent became extinguished.[5] and there was, apparently, no equity to relieve against this result. The law upon this point has, however, been altered by sect. 10 of the Law of Property Amendment Act, 1859.[6] which enacts that " the release from a rentcharge of part of the hereditaments charged therewith shall not extinguish the whole rentcharge, but shall operate only to bar the right to recover any part of the rent-charge out of the hereditaments released, without prejudice, nevertheless, to the rights of all persons interested in the hereditaments remaining unreleased and not concurring in or confirming the release."

---

[1] Co. Litt. 267b.
[2] *Ib.* 149b.
[3] *Ib.* 148a.
[4] Lumley on Annuities, p. 305.

[5] 2 Roll. Ab. 414. Co. Litt. 148. Shep. Touch. 345.
[6] 22 & 23 Vict. c. 35.

The above section deals with two cases: first, where part of the lands are released with the concurrence of the owner of the remainder of the lands subject to the rent, and secondly, where such a release is made without the concurrence of such owner, the words of the section "without prejudice," &c., being only applicable to the latter case. The effect of the section, therefore, is that, if the owner of the unreleased land concurs, effect will be given to the intention of the parties, and the unreleased land will remain liable either to the whole, or part, of the rent according to such intention as it may be either expressed or implied.[1] Thus, where A was the landowner, and B, the husband of A, the rentowner, and A and B joined in a conveyance of a moiety of the land, being expressed in the deed to " grant, release, dispose of, and confirm " one moiety of the land, "and all the estate, right, title, interest, property, claim, and demand, whatsoever of them or either of them in, to, and out of, the same premises," it was held that the abovementioned section applied and that, whilst the moiety conveyed was released by the deed, the other moiety remained liable to the entire rent, the Court under the circumstances of the case apparently considering that to have been the intention of the parties.[2]

[1] *Price* v. *John* (1905) 1 Ch [2] *Ib*
    741

But if, on the release of part of lands which are subject to a rent, the owner of the remainder of the lands subject to the rent is not a concurring party, the effect of the section above referred to will be to apportion the rent, so that the non-concurring owner will be liable in future to pay only the proportion of the rent which the value of the unreleased lands bears to the value of the released lands.[1]

If there are two plots, A and B, which are subject to an entire rent, and the owner sells plot A free from the rent, which he charges upon plot B in exoneration of plot A, it is submitted that the owner of plot B has sufficiently " concurred " in the release of plot A from the rent, and that the rentowner could safely release such plot without further concurrence on the part of the owner of plot B or of any successor in title to such plot. It is not, however, clear that this would be so if, upon the sale of plot A, the vendor had simply covenanted to pay the whole rent without charging it upon plot B, at least if the vendor had subsequently parted with the latter plot, for it is not clear that the burden of the exonerating covenant will run with the land.[2]

Release of land which has been previously sold or exonerated from the rent

Sect. 10 of the Law of Property Amendment Act, 1859, only expressly refers to the case of a

Semble Section 10 does not apply where rent owner acquires part of land out

---

[1] *Booth* v *Smith* (No 2) 14 Q.B.D. 318. *Semble* the value is to be ascertained at the date of the release *Hartley* v *Mad-docks* (1899) 2 Ch 199 *Allison* v *Jenkins* (1904) 1 Ir R 341

[2] *Ante* p 34

" release " of part of the land charged from a rent, and it cannot safely be assumed that it has made any alteration of the law as to the owner of the rent acquiring part of the land charged. The law upon this point was, and, it is thought, still is, that such acquisition generally operates to extinguish the rent entirely,[1] although, possibly, if the rentowner acquired the land in ignorance that the rent was charged upon it, equity might relieve against the consequences.[2] A distinction has, however, always been drawn between the case where the acquisition of the land arises from act of the rentowner, and where it arises by operation of law. For instance, if the land were to descend to the rentowner as heir-at-law of the landowner, the rent would not be extinguished, but apportioned according to the value of the land descended, for an heir-at-law cannot disclaim.[3] A devisee, however, is under no such disability, and if, therefore, being owner of the rent he accepts a devise of portion of the land charged with it, the entire rent will be extinguished,[4]

---

[1] Co. Litt. 147b.

[2] *Slater* v. *Buck*, Moseley 256.

[3] Co. Litt. 147b, 150a. Gilb. on Rents 156. But, *quære* whether the Land Transfer Act 1897 (60 & 61 Vict. c. 65) may not have altered this rule, at least where the heir has requested a conveyance. At any rate it will be safer to request a conveyance to a nominee for the heir. If part of the land be com-

pulsorily acquired under the Land Clauses Act 1845 (8 & 9 Vict. c. 18) see sects. 116-119 of that Act.

[4] *Dennett* v. *Pass* 1 Bing. N.C. 388. If the rent be secured collaterally upon land other than that out of which the rent issues, the acquisition of the former land by the rentowner will not extinguish the rent. Co. Litt. 147a.

subject to a possible claim to relief from a court
of equity, as above suggested.

It is suggested, however, that the owner of an
entire plot subject to the rent, might, on a conveyance or devise of a portion of the land to the
rentowner, by apt words indicating an intention
to throw the entire rent upon the remaining portion,
save the rent from extinction;[1] but wherever a
conveyance *inter vivos* is contemplated of part of
the land charged to the rentowner, the only safe
course to adopt is for the rentowner in reliance
upon sect. 10 of the Law of Property Act, 1859,
above referred to, to release from the rent the land
intended to be conveyed before taking his conveyance of the land.

If the terre tenant be evicted by title paramount
from part of the land upon which the rent is purported to be charged, whether he will be liable to
continue to pay the whole, or only a proportionate
part of the rent, will depend upon whether the rent
was originally *granted* or *reserved*. Thus, if A,
having a title to Whiteacre, but not to Blackacre, purports to grant to B a rent to issue
out of both estates, Whiteacre will still remain liable to pay the whole rent to B
after A's eviction from Blackacre, for a grant
is construed most strongly against the grantor;[2]

[1] *Eyre* v *Green*, Coll C C 527
cf *Grigby* v *Powell* 5 Sim 290,
3 Cl & Fin 103 *Knight* v
Calthorpe 1 Vern 347.

[2] Co Litt 148b

but if A were, in such a case, to purport to convey Whiteacre and Blackacre to B, reserving to himself a rent, B, after eviction from Blackacre, would only be liable to pay a proportionate amount of the rent in respect of Whiteacre.[1] In a recent case, Cozens Hardy J held that if land be conveyed by a vendor in consideration of a rent, and the rent is limited by way of use to the vendor, this is practically a reservation of the rent to the vendor, and that, consequently, if the purchaser is in such a case evicted from part of the land purported to be conveyed, the rent ought to be apportioned, and that the proper basis of apportionment should be according to the respective values of the land to which the vendor had a good title, and of the land to which he had no title, and not according to their respective acreages.[2]

A rentcharge, other than a rent reserved on a sale or lease, or made payable under a grant or licence for building purposes, may be redeemed under sect. 45 of the Conveyancing Act, 1881,[3] at the request of the owner of the land or any person interested therein, made to the Board of Agriculture. The Board certifies the amount of money in consideration whereof the rent may be redeemed, and upon tender of this amount to the person entitled to the fee simple in the rent, or the person empowered

---

[1] Ib

[2] *Hartley v Maddocks* (1899) 2 Ch 199 *Allison v Jenkins* (1904) 1 Ir Rep 341 *Ley v Ley*, L R 6 Eq 174

[3] 44 & 45 Vict c 41

to dispose thereof absolutely, or to give an absolute discharge for the capital value thereof, the Board gives a certificate to the effect that the rent is redeemed, which certificate is to be conclusive. If there is no person entitled to the rent in fee simple or empowered to dispose of it absolutely, or to give an absolute discharge for its capital value, the section would not appear to apply: but, *semble*, trustees for the purposes of the Settled Land Acts are persons able to give such an absolute discharge.[1] It is not very clear what is the meaning of the exception of a rent " reserved on a sale," but, presumably, it is intended to apply only to the case of a sale of land in consideration of a rent, and not to a sale of a rent to be created, the word " reservation " hardly appearing apt to cover a grant of a rent It would, therefore, seem that such a rent could be redeemed under this section against the will of the rentowner, and at a price to be fixed, not by the parties, but by the Board of Agriculture, but that a rent created upon the sale of land could not be so redeemed.

It is the general opinion that the powers conferred upon the Court by sect 5 of the Conveyancing Act, 1881,[2] to direct payment into Court of a sum sufficient to redeem an " incumbrance ' upon a sale of land, do not apply to a perpetual rentcharge,

Quaere whether sect 5 of the Conveyancing Act applies to a rent in fee

---

[1] *Re Hobson's Trusts* 7 Ch D 708 *re Wooton* W N 1890 p 158 *re Torry Hill* (1909) 1 Ch 468

[2] 44 & 45 Vict c 41

and this appears to have been the opinion of Pearson J. in the case of *re Great Northern Railway Company & Sanderson*,[1] although it has been held[2] that a rentcharge is an "incumbrance" within the meaning of sect. 5 of the Settled Land Act, 1882[3] But whether a rentcharge is covered or not by the provisions of sect. 5 of the Conveyancing Act, the powers of that section are discretionary, and, it is thought, not likely to be exercised to effect the redemption of a perpetual rentcharge not otherwise redeemable.

Statutes of Limitation.

The next method by which a rent may be extinguished is by the operation of the Statutes of Limitation. It is provided by sect. 1 of the Real Property Limitation Act, 1874,[4] substituted for sect. 2 of the Act of 1833,[5] that an entry, distress, or action to recover "rent,"[6] must be made or brought within twelve years after the right to make such entry or distress or to bring such action shall have first accrued.[7] This section

---

[1] 25 Ch D 788 See also Copinger, pp 535 536

[2] *Re Shafford & Maples* (1896) 1 Ch 235 It seems to follow that a rentcharge is an "incumbrance" within sect 21 (ii) of the Settled Land Act 1881 upon redemption of which capital moneys may be spent

[3] 45 & 46 Vict c 38 There is, however in the Settled Land Act no definition of incumbrance similar to the definition in sect 2 of the Conveyancing Act 1881

[4] 37 & 38 Vict c 57

[5] 3 & 4 Will IV c 27

[6] This expression does not include rent reserved upon a lease *Grant v Ellis* 9 M & W 113 *Dean of Ely v Cash* 15 M & W 617 *Doe v Angell* 9 Q B 328

[7] Additional time is allowed to remaindermen and persons under disability (ss 2 & 3 of the Act of 1874) and an acknowledgment of title stops the running of the Statute (s 14 of the Act of 1833)

must, however, be read in conjunction with
sect. 3 of the Act of 1833, whereby it is provided
(1) that in the case of a person who has been in
receipt of a rent, but who has been dispossessed
or discontinued receipt, his right of entry, distress,
or action is to be deemed to have first accrued
" at the last time at which any such rent was so
received "; (2) that in the case of the death of a
person entitled to a rent who shall have continued
in receipt thereof down to the date of his death,
but no person shall have received the rent since,
such right shall be deemed to have first accrued
" at the time of such death "; and (3) that in
the case of a person claiming a rent in respect
of an estate or interest in possession assured
by any instrument (other than a will) to him or
some person through whom he claims by a person
who was, in respect of the same estate or interest,
in receipt of the rent, and no person entitled under
such instrument shall have been in such receipt,
such right shall be deemed to have first accrued
' at the time at which the person claiming as aforesaid or the person through whom he claims became
entitled to such receipt by virtue of such instrument

The effect of the above provisions is as follows :
First. If a rentowner has been in receipt of a rent,
but has ceased to receive it, time runs against him,
not from the date when he first had a right to
receive a further payment of rent, but from the
date of his last actual receipt. Thus, if the rent

be payable annually he will be statute barred in, practically, eleven years.[1]

Secondly, if the rentowner has never himself been in receipt of the rent, but derives title through a person who has been in such receipt either (*a*) under a will or intestacy, or (*b*) under a deed or instrument other than a will, he will be statute barred, in the former case twelve years after the death of the testator or intestate, and in the latter case twelve years after the time when he first became entitled to receive the rent, which, presumably, means the date, not when the deed or instrument was executed, but when the first payment thereafter fell due.

Thirdly, if the rentowner claims a rent newly created, whether by deed or will, but which has never been paid, none of the branches of sec. 3 of the Act of 1833 above referred to seems to apply, but time appears to run against the rentowner under sect. 1 of the Act of 1874 from the date when his right of action or distress first accrued, *i.e.*, from the date when the first payment fell due.

Rents created by way of indemnity

This last point has an important bearing upon the efficacy of rents created by way of indemnity. As pointed out in a former chapter,[2] the usual practice in limiting a rent by way of indemnity is to make the rent commence at once, but to pro-

---

[1] *Owen v. De Beauvoir* 16 M & W 547 *Earl of Chichester v. Hall*, 17 L J O S 121 cf   *Zouch v. Dalbiac* L R 10 Exch 172   [2] Ante p 51

vide that it is only to be payable upon the happening of the event against which it is to be a security. Such rents, it is submitted, are not liable to become statute barred until twelve years after the happening of such event.

If the rentowner fails to receive his rent during the statutory period, his title thereto will be extinguished under sect. 34 of the Act of 1833. If during the statutory period the rent has been paid to a person who had no title, such person will, presumably, acquire a title to the rent by virtue of the Statute, but if during such period the rent has been paid to nobody it will be extinguished in favour of the inheritance. A doubt was, indeed, suggested in one case[1] upon this latter point, but it is clear there is no foundation for the doubt.[2]

The Statutes of Limitation do not run against a rentowner until he "discontinues" receipt, and consequently neither the land charged, nor any part thereof, will become freed from the rent if the rentowner has actually received his rent during the statutory period, even though it has been paid during that period by the owner of part only of the land out of which the rent issues.[3]

Consequences of rent owner being statute barred

Rent owner not statute barred if he receives his rent from anyone

---

[1] *Hanks v Filling,* 6 Ell & Bl 659

[2] *Owen v De Beauvoir,* 16 M & W 547 *Irish Commissioners v Grant* 10 A C 14 *Jones v Withers* 74 L T 572 and cf *Chichester v Hall,* 17 L T O S 121 *Howitt v Harrington* (1893) 2 Ch 497

[3] *Woodcock v Titterton* 12 W R 865 *Archbishop of Dublin v Trimleston,* 12 Ir Eq R 251

or even by a person who was under no obligation whatever to pay it.[1]

Long
receipt of
rent may
raise pre-
sumption
of a lost
grant. There is nothing in the Statutes of Limitation to create a rentcharge which has no actual existence, and rentcharges are expressly excepted from sect. 1 of the Prescription 1832.[2] If, however, a person can show twenty years' uninterrupted receipt of a sum paid as rent, and such receipt is uncontradicted and unexplained, this will be evidence from which the Court might presume a lost grant of a rentcharge.[3]

Whether
land-
owner can
be sued
upon his
covenant
after the
rent has
become
extin-
guished In the case of *Manning* v. *Phelps*,[4] where a rentcharge had not been paid during the statutory period, it was held that the terre tenant still remained liable upon the covenant to pay, contained in the deed creating the rent. Unfortunately, the judges who decided this case gave no reasons for their decision, and it is submitted that it cannot be sustained, and that a man can no more sue for arrears of a rentcharge that has been extinguished than for arrears of interest upon a capital debt that has become extinguished[5] A decision contrary to *Manning* v *Phelps* was arrived

---

[1] *Adnam* v *Sandwich* 2 Q B D 485, *Irish Land Commissioners* v *White* (1896) 2 Ir R 410

[2] 3 & 4 Will IV c 71

Bright v *Walker*, 1 C M & R 217 *ex parte McDowal* 5 Jur N S 553 *Bamford* v *Neville* (1904) 1 Ir R 474 And see *Collet* v *Jaques* 1 Ch C 129

Bridgwater v *Edward* 6 Bro P C 368 *Smiles* v *Sanders*, 19 Ch D 373

[5] 10 Exch 59 and see *Paget* v *Foley* 2 Bing N C 679

See per Sugden L C *Henry* v *Smith* 2 Dr & War 381 384, *Hollis* v *Palmer* 2 Bing N C 713

at in Ireland,[1] but *Manning v. Phelps* does not appear to have been cited. Nevertheless the reasoning of the Court of Appeal in *Sutton v Sutton*,[2] which decided that a mortgagee of land is, after twelve years, barred not only in respect of his rights against the land, but also in respect of his rights under the covenant to pay principal and interest, seems clearly to support the view contended for, namely, that when the right to recover a rentcharge against the land is extinguished the right to sue upon the covenant to pay is also extinguished.

It is, however, thought that the covenant to pay the rentcharge may possibly assist in a case where the rentowner has failed to receive his rent for more than six, but less than 12 years. By virtue of sect. 42 of the Real Property Limitation Act, 1883,[3] a rentowner is limited to six years' arrears of rent against the land; but it was held by North J. in the case of *Darley v. Tennant*,[4] upon the authority of *Hunter v Nockolds*,[5] that though the section above referred to deprived a lessor of his right to distrain upon the land for more than six years' arrears, yet he might recover 20 years arrears of royalties in an action upon the covenant for payment. This was a case of land-

[1] *Re Nugents Trusts* 19 L R Ir 140 *Fearnsides Trust* 22 Ch D 581 *re Frisby* 43 Ch D 106
[2] 22 Ch D 511
[3] 3 & 4 Will IV c 27
[4] 53 L T 257

[5] 1 Mac & G 640 This case, however, appears to have been treated by the Court in *re Nugents Trusts* (supra) as over ruled by *Sutton v Sutton* (supra)

lord and tenant, but the reasoning would seem to apply to arrears of a rentcharge, so long as the rentcharge remains unextinguished.[1] It is true that North J. appears to have suggested that the royalties were not charged upon the land within the meaning of sect. 42 of the Act,[2] but in an Irish case,[3] it has been held that a lessor could recover 20 years' arrears of ordinary rent upon the covenant. The point, however, must be considered doubtful.

Again, sect. 42 of the Real Property Limitation Act, 1833, is confined to the case where the rent-owner is seeking to enforce payment of the arrears of his rent by "distress, action, or suit," and it may be that the rentowner can obtain more than six years arrears of rent under his power of entry for perception of rents and profits—provided, of course, that the rent has not become extinguished —although if the rentowner were to enforce his power of absolute re-entry the terre tenant might perhaps obtain relief from forfeiture on payment of six years' arrears of rent.[4]

The Statutes of Limitation and powers of entry

Entry by a rentowner under a power of absolute re-entry will extinguish the rent, and if he enters under a void power he will acquire a title to the

---

[1] The title of a lessor is not extinguished by non payment of the rent during the currency of the lease *Doe v Oxenham* 7 M & W 131

[2] See *Paget v Foley* 2 Bing N C 679

[3] *Donegan v Neill* 16 L R Ir 309

[4] *Percival v Dunn* 9 Ir C L R 422 *Sed quære see Dingle v Coppen* (1899) 1 Ch 726 an l *re Lloyd* (1903) 1 Ch 385

land in 12 years under the Real Property Limitation Act, 1874 :[2] but the impression that a rentowner who enters under a power of entry for perception of rents and profits, and holds without acknowledgment of the landowner's title for over 12 years, thereby acquires a title under the Statute of Limitations, is erroneous. The rentowner's possession is lawful under such circumstances, and under sect. 1 of the Real Property Limitation Act, 1874,[2] time will not begin to run against the *terre* tenant until he has a right to possession—that is to say, until the rentowner has been satisfied of his rent—and inasmuch as the right to the rent, and consequently the right for the rentowner to be in possession, periodically recurs, the rentowner will be unable to acquire a statutory title to the land, however long he may have been in possession, under a power of entry for perception of rents and profits, and even although the profits may have been more than sufficient to keep down the arrears of rentcharge.[1]

[1] 3 & 4 Will IV c 27   [2] Cf *re Harris* (1901) 1 Ch. 931

APPENDIX.

REFERENCES TO PRECEDENTS

[Pr. Prideaux's Precedents (19th ed.) K. & L. Key
and Elphinstone's Precedents (8th ed.) Enc. En-
cyclopædia of Forms and Precedents Dav. Davidson's
Precedents Byth. & J. Bythewood and Jarman (4th
ed.) Cop. Coppinger and Munro on Rents Dav.
Con. Davidson's Concise Precedents Farrer Farrer's Conditions of Sale (2nd ed.)]

AGREEMENTS AND CONDITIONS OF SALE

Agreement for sale of land in consideration of a rent 1
B. & J. 156 1 K. & L. 358 12 Enc. 212, 215 Cop.
616 619

Conditions of sale of land in consideration of a rent Farrer
219 1 K. & L. 336

Agreement for sale of land subject to existing rent 12 Enc.
187 1 Pr. 218

Conditions of sale of land subject to existing rent 1 K. & L.
339 Farrer 115 117

Agreement for sale of land for a sum in gross and a perpetual
rent the purchaser being indemnified against a pre-
existing smaller rent 1 K. & L. 358

Special conditions on sale of part of land subject to a rent
1 K. & L. 191 1 Dav. 551 et seq. 12 Enc. 369 373

Agreement for sale of a rent to be created 1 Enc. 513 Cop.
615

Conditions of sale of existing rent 1 K. & L. 333 1 Enc.
557 Cop. 657 Farrer 215

CONVEYANCES

Conveyance by fee simple owner in consideration of a rent charge, 1 Pr. 129, 138 · 2 Dav. Pt. I 501 · Dav. Conc 205 · 5 B. & J. 555 · 12 Enc. 598 · 1 K. & E. 592.

Conveyance by tenant for life in consideration of a rent, 1 Pr. 133 131 · 12 Enc. 631 *et seq* · Wolstenholme's Precedents (6th ed.) 350 · 1 K. & E. 595

Conveyance by trustees in consideration of a rent, 12 Enc. 636

Conveyance by mortgagor and mortgagee in consideration of a rent substituted as security, 1 K. & E. 598 · 1 Pr. 135 · 12 Enc. 647 649

Conveyance of land subject to an existing rent, Dav. Conc 213 · 5 B. & J. 561 · 1 Pr. 136 · 12 Enc. 595

Conveyance in consideration of a second rent, 12 Enc. 640 Cop. 680

Mortgage of land subject to a rent, 2 Dav. Pt. II 581 · 8 Enc. 529

Conveyance of part of land subject to a rent, 1 Pr. 139 140 · 12 Enc. 642 *et seq* · 1 K. & E. 592 · 5 B. & J. 566 Cop. 681 *et seq* (and see form given in full below)

Apportionment of rents, 2 Enc. 14 *et seq* · 5 Dav. Pt. II 24 · 1 K. & L. 57 · 2 K. & L. 312 · 1 Pr. 143

Conveyance in fee of first rent, 1 Enc. 562 · 1 Pr. 137 · Cop 690 · 1 K. & L. 599 · 5 B. & J. 562

Conveyance in fee of second rent, 1 Enc. 563 · Cop 691

Mortgage of a first rent, 8 Enc. 667 · Cop 694

Mortgage of a second rent, 8 Enc. 669

Grant of rent in fee, 1 Enc. 545, 547 549 · Cop. 662, 663 664

Release of a rent, 2 K. & E. 407 · 1 Pr. 115 · 6 B. & J. 62 1 Enc. 569 · 11 Enc. 197 · Cop 695

Conveyance to two purchasers of two plots of land subject to an appointed part of a rent of £28. 10s. (the vendor himself retaining a third plot) with cross powers of entry and distress, the plots being subject with other land, to an overriding rent of £69. 10s

THIS INDENTURE dated &c. and made between W. H. of &c. (*the vendor*) of the 1st part, A. B. of &c. (*first purchaser*) of the 2nd part and J. L. of &c. (*second purchaser*) of the 3rd part.

WHEREAS by an Indenture dated the 1st day of March 1882 and made between &c. the hereditaments described in the 1st Schedule hereto (being a plot of land which included the hereditaments assured by the Indenture next hereinafter recited) were assured to uses limiting to one X. Y. and his heirs a perpetual yearly rentcharge of £69. 10s. and subject thereto and to the powers and remedies for the recovery thereof to the use of S. M. in fee simple. And in the said Indenture are contained certain covenants by the said S. M. and conditions to be performed and observed as to buildings and otherwise

AND WHEREAS by an Indenture dated the 4th day of July 1882 and made between the said S. M. of the one part and the said W. H. of the other part the hereditaments described in the 2nd Schedule hereto (being portion of the hereditaments comprised in the hereinbefore recited Indenture of the 1st day of March 1882 and including the hereditaments intended to be hereby assured) were assured by the said S. M. to the use that the said S. M. and his heirs should receive thereout a perpetual yearly rentcharge of £28. 10s. and subject thereto and to the powers and remedies for the recovery thereof to the use of the said W. H. in fee simple and the Indenture now in recital contained covenants by the said S. M. for payment of the said rent of £69. 10s. and for indemnity against the same or any breach of the grantee's

covenants contained in the hereinbefore recited Indenture of
the 1st day of March, 1882, except so far as the same related
to the hereditaments assured by the Indenture now in recital
and power was given to the said W. H. his heirs and assigns
in the event of his or their being called upon to pay the said
rent of £69 10s. or any part thereof or in the event of his or
their suffering any loss by reason of the exercise of any powers
of entry for distress or perception of rents and profits over
the hereditaments by the said Indenture now in recital assured
to retain the said rent of £28 10s. and further that he or
they should have powers of entry for distress and perception of rents and profits over the land coloured blue on the
Indenture now in recital and edged blue on the plan drawn
on these presents

AND WHEREAS the said W. H. has agreed with the
said A B for the sale to him for an estate in fee simple in
possession free from incumbrances of the hereditaments
first hereinafter described and intended to be hereby assured
(being part of the hereditaments comprised in the herein
before recited Indentures of the 1st day of March 1882 and
4th day of July 1882) subject to a yearly rentcharge of
£9 10s. as an apportioned part of the said yearly rentcharge
of £28 10s. and to the grantee's covenants and conditions
in the said Indenture of the 4th day of July 1882 contained
so far as the same relate to such hereditaments at the price
of £500

[*Recite similar contract with J L subject to a similar apportioned
rent*]

NOW THIS INDENTURE WITNESSETH that in pur-
suance of the said agreement and in consideration of the
sum of £500 now paid by the said A B to the said W H
(the receipt whereof is hereby acknowledged) the said W H
as Beneficial Owner hereby grants and conveys unto the

I

said A. B. ALL &c. (*parcels*) and also the full benefit and ad
vantage in common with the said W. H. of the covenants
by the said S. M. contained in the hereinbefore recited In
denture of the 4th day of July 1882 for payment of the
said yearly rentcharge of £69. 10s. and for indemnity against
the same and against any breach of the covenants and conditions in the hereinbefore recited Indenture of the 1st day
of March 1882 contained except so far as the same relate
to the hereditaments comprised in the hereinbefore recited
Indenture of the 4th day of July 1882 and also of the powers
in the last mentioned Indenture contained of retention and
of entry for distress and perception of rents and profits over
the land edged blue on the said plan drawn on these presents
by way of further indemnity against the said yearly rent
charge of £69. 10s. and against any damages or expenses
occasioned to the said A. B. his heirs or assigns by reason of
the non payment thereof or of the exercise by the owner
or owners of the said yearly rentcharge of £69. 10s. of any
powers of entry for distress or perception of rents and profits
over the land hereby granted and assured to the said A. B.

TO HOLD the premises unto and to the use of the said
A. B. his heirs and assigns subject nevertheless to the yearly
rentcharge or sum of £9. 10s. as an apportioned part of the
said yearly rentcharge of £28. 10s. and to the covenants and
conditions in the hereinbefore recited Indentures of the 1st
day of March 1882 and 4th day of July 1882 respectively
contained so far as the same respectively relate to the hereditaments hereinbefore expressed to be hereby assured

AND THE INDENTURE ALSO WITNESSETH [*similar
conveyance to J. L.*]

AND the said A. B. for himself and his assigns hereby
covenants with the said W. H. and J. L. respectively that he
the said A. B. his heirs or assigns will henceforth pay the said
yearly rentcharge or sum of £9. 10s. the proportionate part

of the said yearly rentcharge of £28. 10s. limited and made payable by the hereinbefore recited Indenture of the 4th day of July 1882 and perform and observe all the grantee's covenants and conditions contained in the same Indenture and in the said Indenture of the 1st day of March 1882 respectively and henceforth to be observed and performed so far as the same respectively relate to the hereditaments hereinbefore expressed to be hereby conveyed to the said A B. and will at all times keep the said W H and J L respectively their respective heirs executors administrators and assigns and such of the premises comprised in the said Indenture of the 4th day of July 1882 as are not hereinbefore expressed to be hereby conveyed to the said A B. indemnified against all actions proceedings costs damages claims demands or liability for non-payment of the last mentioned yearly rentcharge or sum of £9. 10s or any part thereof or the breach or non performance or non observance of the said covenants and conditions or any of them so far as the same relate to the hereditaments hereinbefore expressed to be hereby conveyed to the said A B [*Similar covenant by J L. with W. H and A B.*]

AND the said W H hereby subjects and charges such portions of the hereditaments as are comprised in the hereinbefore recited Indenture of the 4th day of July 1882 and not hereby conveyed respectively and which hereditaments are coloured yellow on the plan drawn on these presents with the payment of the yearly rentcharge or sum of £9 10s being the remaining portion of the said yearly rentcharge of £28 10s limited and made payable by the said Indenture of the 4th day of July 1882 and with the performance and observance of the covenants and conditions in the same Indenture and also in the said Indenture of the 1st day of March 1882 respectively contained and henceforth to be performed and observed so far as the same relate to the hereditaments comprised in the said Indenture of the 4th day of July 1882 and not hereby respectively conveyed

*[Covenant by W. H. with A. B. and J. L. to pay his apportioned
rent as before.]*

AND each of them the said W. H. A. B. and J. L. hereby
grants to the others and other of them their and his heirs
and assigns that if default shall be made in payment of the
respective proportions of the said yearly rentcharge or any
part or parts thereof subject to which the said respective
portions of land comprised in the said Indenture of the 4th
day of July 1882 have become chargeable by virtue of these
presents after any of the days by the said last mentioned
Indenture appointed for payment of the said yearly rentcharge of £28 10s [1] or there shall be a breach of any of the
covenants or conditions therein or in the said Indenture of the
1st day of March 1882 contained on the part of any of them
then and in any and every such case it shall be lawful for
the others or other of them their or his heirs or assigns into
and upon the premises in respect of which such default or
breach shall have occurred or any part or parts thereof to enter
and distrain and the distress or distresses then and there
found to dispose of in due course according to law and also to
enter into and upon and to hold the said premises in respect
whereof such default or breach as aforesaid shall have occurred
or any part or parts thereof and to take and hold the rents
and profits thereof until by the means aforesaid or some of
them or otherwise the yearly rent or sum so unpaid and
all costs and expenses incurred by reason of such default
or breach shall have been wholly paid and satisfied such
possession when taken to be without impeachment of waste

---

[1] Sometimes the form is altered so as to give the powers of entry
and distress only after the rentowner has required payment from the
owner of any plot of more than his proper proportion of the rent
but in this case the form in the text is, it is submitted reasonable
Where a rent is apportioned the frequent practice is for one to collect
the apportioned parts and pay the entire rent to the rentowner

[PROVIDED ALWAYS that the powers of entry for distress and perception of rents and profits hereinbefore contained shall be exerciseable only during the lifetime of the descendants now living of her late Majesty Queen Victoria and during the lifetime of the survivor of them and during twenty one years after the death of such survivor and during such further period as may not be contrary to the law against perpetuities][1]

AND the said W. H hereby acknowledges the right of the said A. B. and J. L. and each of them to production of the hereinbefore recited Indentures of the 1st day of March 1882 and 4th day of July 1882 and to delivery of copies thereof respectively and hereby undertakes for the safe custody thereof respectively

IN WITNESS, &c

[SCHEDULES]

---

[1] The power of entry being given in this case for breach of the covenants as well as for non payment of the apportioned rent, must, it is thought, be confined within the perpetuity period. See ante p 16

INDEX.

Printed by TAYLOR, GARNETT, EVANS & CO LTD
Manchester, London and Reddish